This book belongs to:

In every thing by prayer and supplication with
thanksgiving let your requests be made known
unto God. And the peace of God, which passeth
all understanding, shall keep your hearts
and minds through Jesus Christ.

— PHILLIPIANS 4:6-7

LEISURE ARTS, INC.
Little Rock, Arkansas

EDITORIAL STAFF

Vice President and Editor-in-Chief: Anne Van Wagner Childs. *Executive Director:* Sandra Graham Case. *Editorial Director:* Susan Frantz Wiles. *Publications Director:* Carla Bentley. *Creative Art Director:* Gloria Bearden. *Senior Graphics Art Director:* Melinda Stout. PRODUCTION — *Managing Editor:* Susan White Sullivan. *Senior Editor:* Andrea Ahlen. *Project Coordinators:* Stephanie Gail Sharp and Jennifer S. Potts. DESIGN — *Design Director:* Patricia Wallenfang Sowers. EDITORIAL — *Managing Editor:* Linda L. Trimble. *Associate Editor:* Terri Leming Davidson. *Assistant Editors:* Tammi Williamson Bradley, Robyn Sheffield-Edwards, Darla Burdette Kelsay, and Andrea Isaac Adams. *Copy Editor:* Laura Lee Weland. ART — *Book/Magazine Graphics Art Director:* Diane M. Hugo. *Senior Graphics Illustrator:* Stephen L. Mooningham. *Graphics Illustrators:* Fred Bassett, Faith R. Lloyd, and Dana M. Morris. *Photography Stylists:* Pam Choate, Sondra Daniel, Karen Hall, Aurora Huston, Courtney Jones, Christina Tiano Myers, and Bridgett Shrum. PROMOTIONS — *Managing Editors:* Tena Kelley Vaughn and Marjorie Ann Lacy. *Associate Editors:* Steven M. Cooper, Dixie L. Morris, and Jennifer Ertl. *Designers:* Dale Rowett and Rhonda H. Hestir. *Art Directors:* Jeff Curtis and Linda Lovette Smart. *Production Artist:* Leslie Loring Krebs. *Publishing Systems Administrator:* Cindy Lumpkin. *Publishing Systems Assistant:* Susan M. Gray.

BUSINESS STAFF

Publisher: Bruce Akin. *Vice President, Finance:* Tom Siebenmorgen. *Vice President, Retail Sales:* Thomas L. Carlisle. *Retail Sales Director:* Richard Tignor. *Vice President, Retail Marketing:* Pam Stebbins. *Retail Marketing Director:* Margaret Sweetin. *Retail Customer Services Manager:* Carolyn Pruss. *General Merchandise Manager:* Russ Barnett. *Distribution Director:* Ed M. Strackbein. *Vice President, Marketing:* Guy A. Crossley. *Marketing Manager:* Byron L. Taylor. *Print Production Manager:* Laura Lockhart.

CREDITS

PHOTOGRAPHY: Ken West, Larry Pennington, and Karen Busick Shirey of Peerless Photography, Little Rock, Arkansas; and Jerry R. Davis of Jerry Davis Photography, Little Rock, Arkansas. COLOR SEPARATIONS: Magna IV Color Imaging of Little Rock, Arkansas.

Library of Congress Catalog Number 96-77626
International Standard Book Number 1-57486-047-X

INTRODUCTION

As children of God, we are indeed blessed with the privilege of prayer — that personal time of worship when we lift up our hearts to the Lord, praising His goodness, interceding for others, and revealing our own needs. Such moments of divine fellowship restore our souls and empower us with His grace. In Let Us Pray, an uplifting volume of hand-stitched eloquence, we celebrate the timeless scriptures and poetic verses that enrich our daily communion with the Father. Many of these poignant cross-stitched designs were adapted from vintage lithographs and cherished paintings, including several stirring portraits of Jesus during His earthly ministry. Other images honor the many heavenly gifts we enjoy each day: a garden's bounty, our family's love, and the joy of children. As you review this splendid collection of heirlooms, may you discover a wealth of blessings that will inspire your walk with God.

TABLE OF CONTENTS

JESUS AT GETHSEMANE

Then cometh Jesus with them unto a place called Gethsemane, and saith unto the disciples, Sit ye here, while I go and pray yonder. ... And he went a little farther, and fell on his face, and prayed, saying, O my Father, if it be possible, let this cup pass from me: nevertheless not as I will, but as thou wilt.

— MATTHEW 26:36, 39

Chart on pages 50-51

COME, LITTLE CHILDREN

With welcoming arms, Jesus bids the little children to follow their hearts and come unto Him. As these beloved lambs seek his fellowship, the Lord secures them in the promise of His kingdom, for all the children of the world are truly precious in His sight.

Chart on pages 52-53

FLOWERS OF FAITH

Following the bleak months of winter, God fills the earth with resplendent blossoms, bringing the promise of spring to us once again. We rejoice in these fragrant gifts and give thanks for the wondrous miracles that the Lord has made.

This is the day which the Lord hath made.

Psalm 118:24

Charts on pages 58 and 59

For, lo, the winter is past, the rain is over and gone; The flowers appear on the earth; the time of the singing of birds is come. ... O my dove, that art in the clefts of the rock, in the secret places of the stairs, let me see thy countenance, let me hear thy voice; for sweet is thy voice, and thy countenance is comely.

— SONG OF SOLOMON 2:11-12, 14

Chart on page 57

12

Charts on pages 60 and 61

AMAZING GRACE

The familiar strains of Amazing Grace — one of the most beloved hymns of all time — have provided Christians with blessed comfort for more than two centuries. Written by a reformed slave-ship captain, the simple verses of redemption and praise convey the divine forgiveness that awaits even the least of us.

Amazing Grace

How sweet the sound
That saved a wretch like me.
I once was lost but now am found
Was blind but now I see.

'Twas grace that taught my
Heart to fear
And grace my fears relieved.
How precious did that grace appear
The hour I first believed.

When we've been there
Ten thousand years,
Bright shining as the sun,
We've no less days to sing
God's praise
Than when we first begun.

Chart on pages 62-63

heartfelt scriptures

Through our studies of God's word, we often are delighted to discover precious scriptures that speak to our hearts with a divine message. Such cherished passages, tucked in the pages of a Bible or framed for all to see, inspire us to uphold our hopes for the heavenly reward that awaits us.

Charts on pages 54 and 55

HERB GARDEN

One of God's earliest gifts to mankind, fragrant herbs continue to bless us with their beauty and essence. Faithfully we tend the tiny seeds and rejoice as we discover tender sprouts of oregano, lavender, and mint peeking through the earth. We pause, savoring their distinctive aromas, and whisper our thanks to the Provider.

The cross-stitch design reads:

Pleasant words are like a honeycomb

sweetness to the soul and health to the body.
Proverbs 16:24

Chart on pages 66-67

20

*A*bloom with nature's splendor, a discerning sampler reminds
us that, with our words and with our deeds, we plant the seeds of
kindness wherever we go. Thoughtful tokens, seasoned with a variety
of herb motifs, will bring the flavor of friendship to any home.

Charts on pages 64-67

THE 23RD PSALM

Just as a watchful shepherd attends his flock, our Lord diligently loves, protects, and guides each of His children along virtuous paths. At times we may stray, becoming discouraged or frightened, but the Father stands ready to restore our strength and peace. This serene Psalm of David, often recalled in moments of adversity, conveys the constant reassurance we find in our walk with the Good Shepherd.

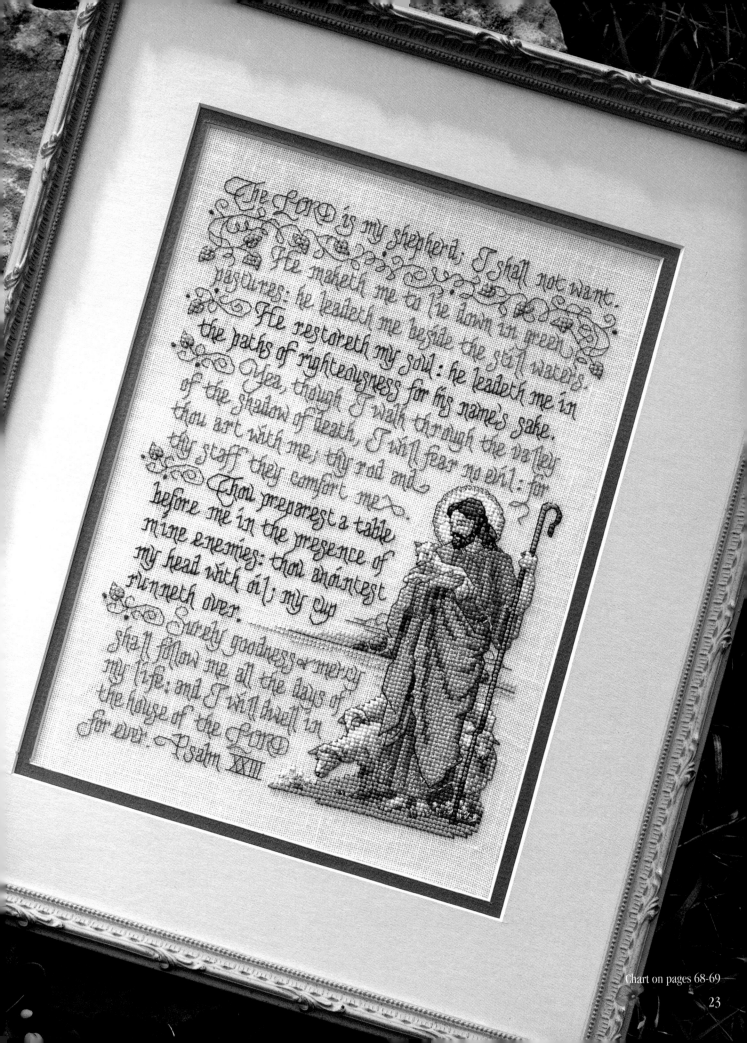

The Lord is my shepherd; I shall not want. He maketh me to lie down in green pastures: he leadeth me beside the still waters. He restoreth my soul: he leadeth me in the paths of righteousness for his name's sake. Yea, though I walk through the valley of the shadow of death, I will fear no evil: for thou art with me; thy rod and thy staff they comfort me. Thou preparest a table before me in the presence of mine enemies: thou anointest my head with oil; my cup runneth over. Surely goodness & mercy shall follow me all the days of my life: and I will dwell in the house of the Lord for ever. ~ Psalm XXIII

Chart on pages 68-69

GUARDIAN ANGEL

Each flitting butterfly and tender blossom holds a world of wonder for inquisitive children. Lost in their fascination, little explorers seldom notice the hidden perils passed along their way, nor do they sense the angelic caresses and whispering wings that shield them from harm.

Chart on pages 70-71

25

THE LOVE OF FAMILY

Through each of life's wondrous milestones, we find our most fulfilling blessings in the devotion of our family. Loved ones are ever near, celebrating in our happiness and providing comfort for our worries. These examples of care guide us as we joyously unite in a new legacy of love.

Love is patient, love is kind, and is not jealous; love does not brag and is not arrogant, does not act unbecomingly; it does not seek its own, is not provoked, does not take into account a wrong suffered, does not rejoice in unrighteousness, but rejoices with the truth; bears all things, believes all things, hopes all things, endures all things. Love never fails. But now abide faith, hope, love, these three; but the greatest of these is love.

I Corinthians
13: 4-8,13

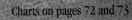
Charts on pages 72 and 73

27

For special couples you hold dear, these tokens offer lovely expressions of your sentiments. A sweet sampler, accented with a border of hearts, will be a cherished wedding day remembrance. Presented to beloved parents, these embellished verses honor Mother and Father on their special days.

Chart on page 74

Charts on page 75

𝒯rain up a child in the way he should go: and when he is old, he will not depart from it.

— PROVERBS 22:6

Chart on pages 76-7

Thow delightful it is to share in the innocent prayers of a child, tiny hands folded and head sweetly bowed. As the little one snuggles under the covers, we can almost sense the Holy Spirit blanketing her in peaceful slumber.

Chart on page 78

Chart on page 78

CHILDREN OF GOD

Kneeling beside a tranquil pool, a little one gazes at her reflection and wonders what her future holds. She is a gem of possibility, free to aspire to any goal as she looks to the Father for His wisdom and direction. Along whatever path she follows, this sweet lass can rest assured that she will always remain a child of God.

For now we see
through a glass, darkly;
but
then
face
to face;
now I know
in part;
but then shall I know
even as also I am known.
I Cor 13:12

Chart on pages 80-81

Take fast hold of Instruction;
let her not go:
keep her;
for she
is
thy
life.

Pro. 4:13

Chart on page 83

*The peals of laughter from lighthearted children, playfully
mimicking our grown-up work, restore the simple pleasures that
can become hidden in our haste. Through the joy they bring us, we
realize that these angels must surely have been sent from above.*

Chart on page 82

MY PRAYER

The reflective moments we spend in prayer allow us to speak to our Lord, conveying to Him the needs He already understands. Although we may not always receive the responses we expect for our requests, our loving Father fulfills His plan through the answers He provides.

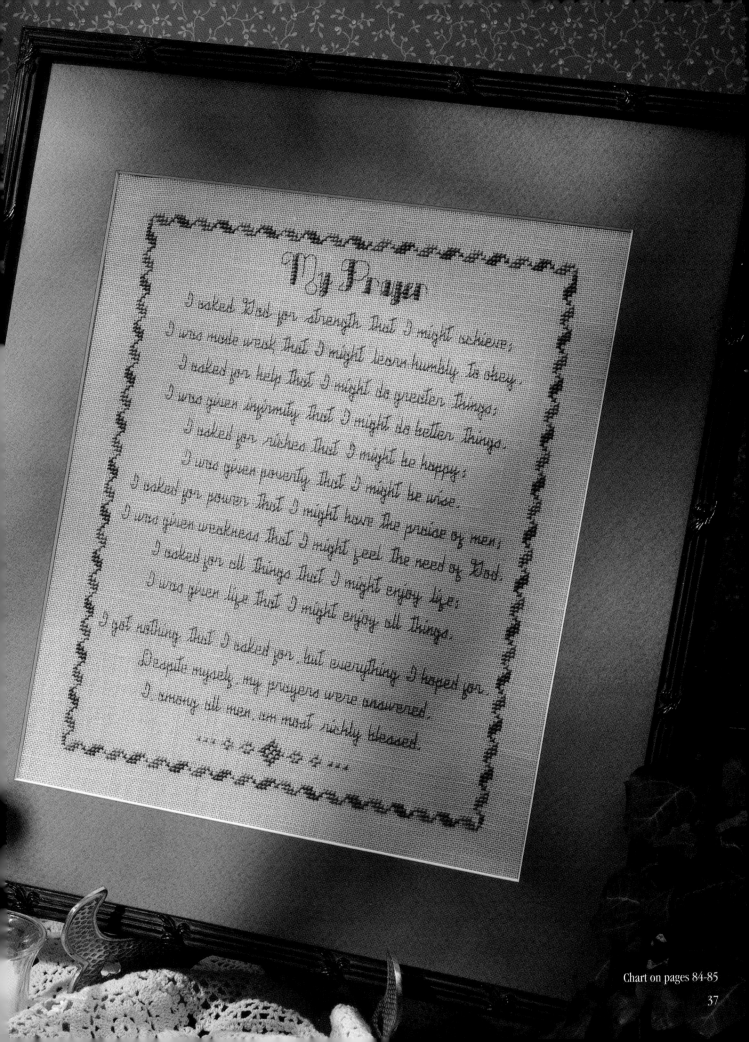

My Prayer

I asked God for strength that I might achieve;
I was made weak that I might learn humbly to obey.
I asked for help that I might do greater things;
I was given infirmity that I might do better things.
I asked for riches that I might be happy;
I was given poverty that I might be wise.
I asked for power that I might have the praise of men;
I was given weakness that I might feel the need of God.
I asked for all things that I might enjoy life;
I was given life that I might enjoy all things.

I got nothing that I asked for, but everything I hoped for.
Despite myself, my prayers were answered.
I, among all men, am most richly blessed.

Chart on pages 84-85

Noah's Ark

In the midst of iniquity, Noah and his family stood alone in their righteousness and thus were spared from the torrential floods that enveloped the earth. God was well pleased with his servant's faithful obedience and promised never again to invoke such wrath upon the land. Unto this day, each beautiful rainbow that graces the sky serves as a reminder of that covenant.

Chart on pages 86-87

ABUNDANT THANKSGIVING

At harvesttime, we are reminded of the abundance that the Lord has so generously bestowed upon us. The Father lovingly provides for His children, nourishing their bodies as well as their spirits. For these gifts, we offer our sincerest gratitude, and recommit ourselves to His service.

GIVE THANKS TO THE LORD
FOR THE LORD IS GOOD, JER. 33:11

Chart on pages 88-89

41

We plough, we sow
the open fields
Till, blest,
each one
its harvest yields,
And unto Him our
thanks we give
Who blesses
so that
we may
live.

Chart on page 90

The blessing of a fruitful harvest is the farmer's greatest reward for his tireless toil. As we read in the Gospel of Luke, Jesus used a parable to illustrate the mission given to His disciples — to sow the message of salvation and reap a bounty of souls in the name of the Lord.

Chart on page 91

CANTICLE OF BROTHER SUN

During his life of quiet contemplation, St. Francis of Assisi taught his followers to cherish the simple gifts from God that are often overlooked in everyday life. The poetic friar found special pleasures in the earth and sky, regarding them as fellow creations. These prayerful verses sing praises for the precious fruits of nature.

Chart on pages 92-93

Lady Liberty

Paul's words to the churches at Galatia offer a special inspiration to Americans. In a nation founded on religious freedom, we can celebrate the spiritual liberty we've found through Jesus Christ.

Stand fast therefore
in the liberty
wherewith Christ
hath set us free.
GAL. 5:1

Chart on page 79

THE LORD'S PRAYER

During His Sermon on the Mount, Christ shared a model upon which our own prayers should be patterned. Our most steadfast concerns should be to honor our Heavenly Father, expressing our faith and hope in His kingdom. Then, by Christ's example, might our daily needs of forgiveness and deliverance be fulfilled.

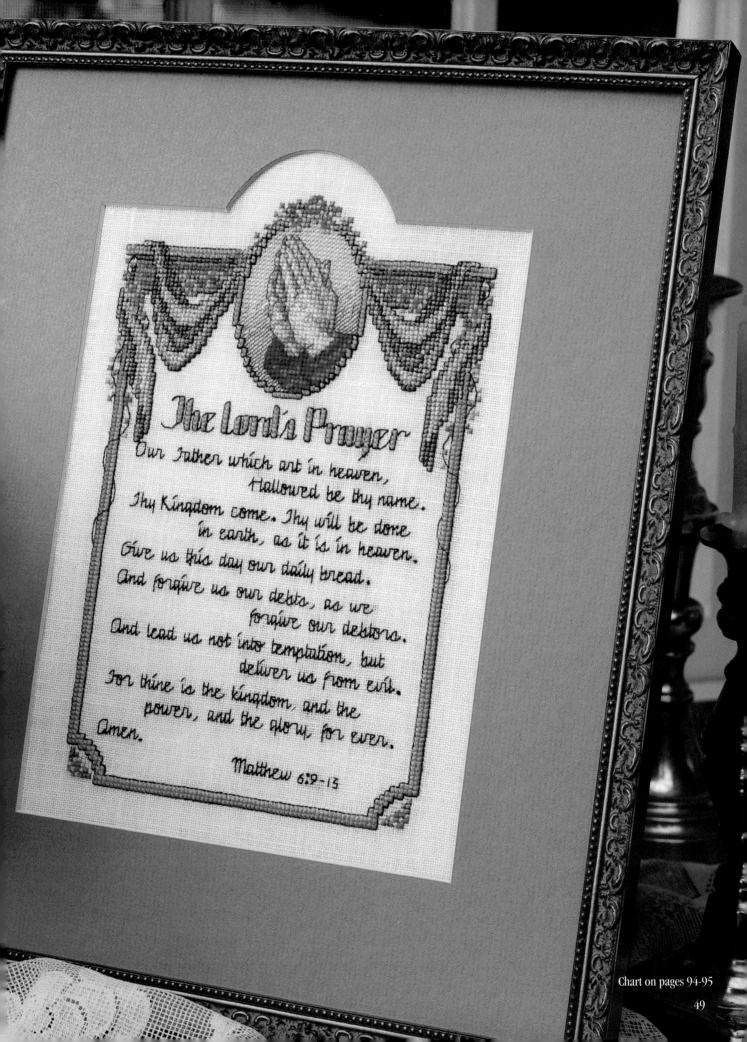

Chart on pages 94-95

JESUS AT GETHSEMANE

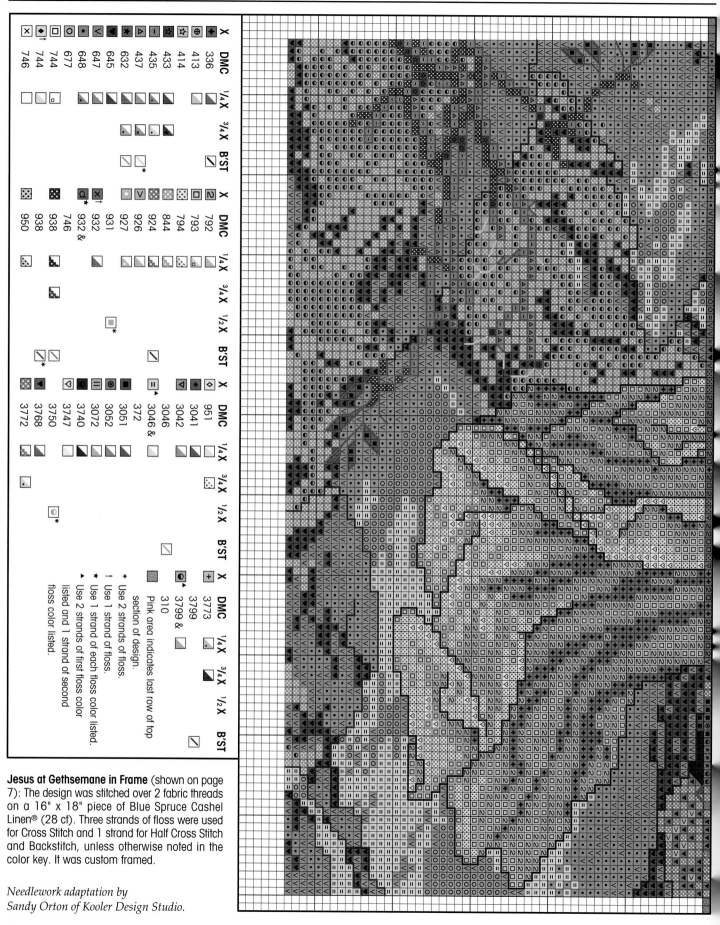

Color Key (DMC):

336, 413, 414, 433, 435, 437, 632, 645, 647, 648, 677, 744, 744, 744, 746

792, 793, 794, 844, 924, 926, 927, 931, 932 &, 932, 938, 938, 746, 950

951, 3041, 3042, 3046 &, 3046, 372, 3051, 3052, 3072, 3740, 3747, 3750, 3768, 3772

3773, 3799, 3799 &, 310

Pink area indicates last row of top section of design.

* Use 2 strands of floss.
† Use 1 strand of floss.
✶ Use 1 strand of each floss color listed.
▶ Use 2 strands of first floss color listed and 1 strand of second floss color listed.

Jesus at Gethsemane in Frame (shown on page 7): The design was stitched over 2 fabric threads on a 16" x 18" piece of Blue Spruce Cashel Linen® (28 ct). Three strands of floss were used for Cross Stitch and 1 strand for Half Cross Stitch and Backstitch, unless otherwise noted in the color key. It was custom framed.

Needlework adaptation by Sandy Orton of Kooler Design Studio.

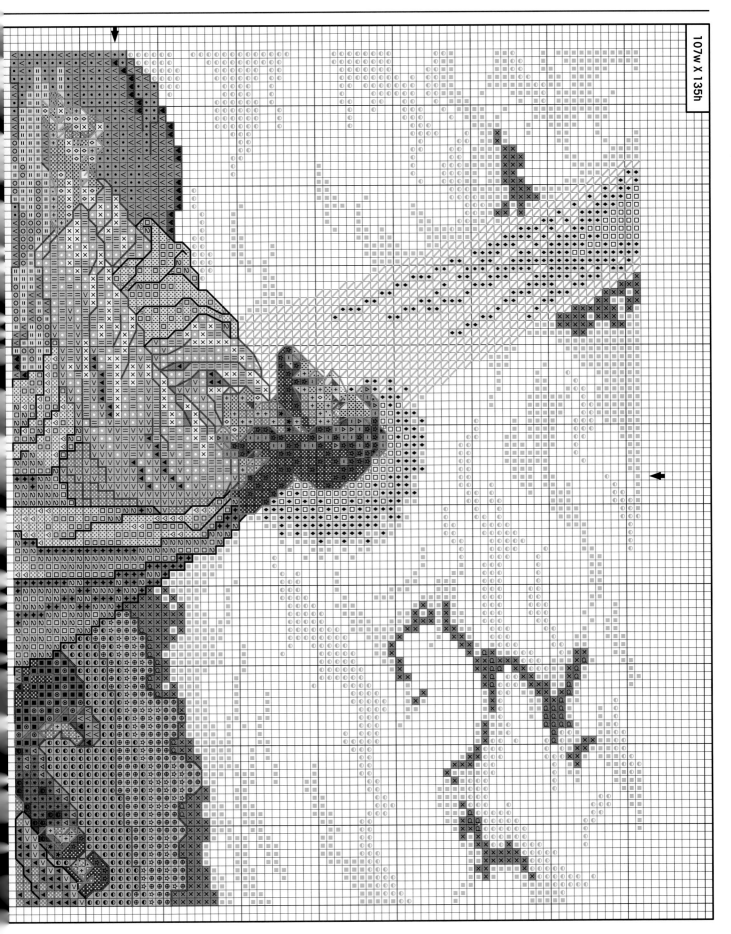

COME, LITTLE CHILDREN

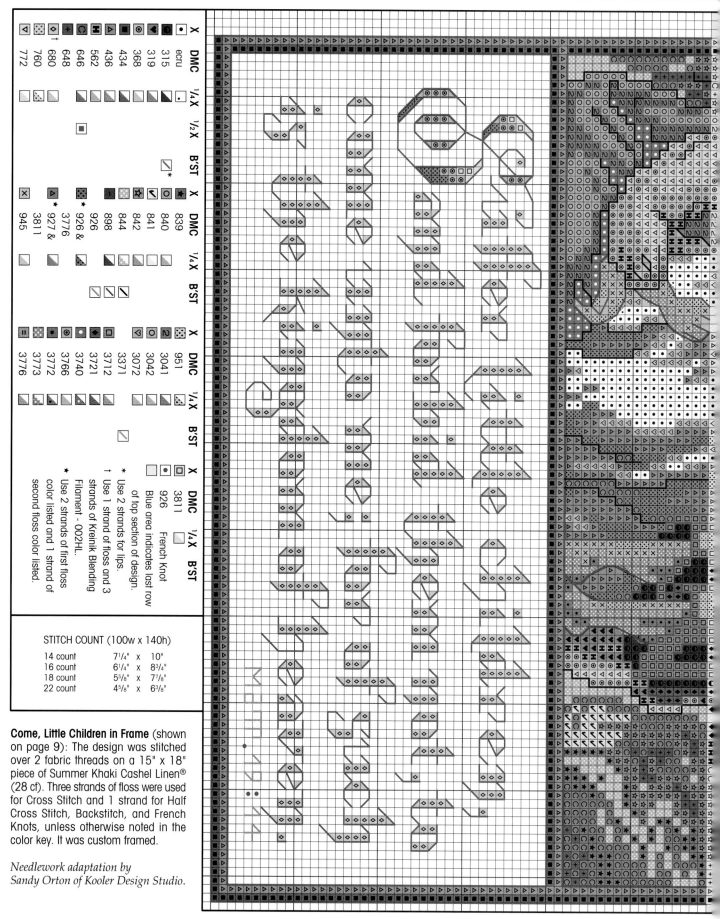

X	DMC	¼X	½X	B'ST
◄	ecru	.		
⊡	315	◨		
⊞	319	◨		
⊞	368	◨		
+	434	◨		
⊙	436	◨		
⊡	562	◨		
▷	646	◨		
■	648	◨		
⊙	680	◨		
◄	760			
◨	772			

X	DMC	¼X	B'ST
	839	◨	
	840	◨	
	841	◨	
	842	◨	
	844	◨	
⊠	898	◨	
▷	926		
⊡	926 &		
★	927 &		
	3776	◨	�%
	3811		
	945	◨	

X	DMC	¼X	B'ST
‖	951	◨	
⊡	3041	◨	
●	3042	◨	
⊙	3072		
◆	3371	◨	
⊡	3712		
◄	3721	◨	
⊡	3740	◨	
2	3766		◨
⊡	3772		
	3773		
	3776		

X	DMC	¼X	B'ST
⊡	3811	◨	
●	926		◨
◻	3811		

French Knot

Blue area indicates last row of top section of design.

* Use 2 strands for lips.
† Use 1 strand of floss and 3 strands of Kreinik Blending Filament - 002HL.
★ Use 2 strands of first floss color listed and 1 strand of second floss color listed.

STITCH COUNT (100w x 140h)

14 count	7¼"	x	10"
16 count	6¼"	x	8¾"
18 count	5⅝"	x	7⅞"
22 count	4⅝"	x	6⅜"

Come, Little Children in Frame (shown on page 9): The design was stitched over 2 fabric threads on a 15" x 18" piece of Summer Khaki Cashel Linen® (28 ct). Three strands of floss were used for Cross Stitch and 1 strand for Half Cross Stitch, Backstitch, and French Knots, unless otherwise noted in the color key. It was custom framed.

Needlework adaptation by Sandy Orton of Kooler Design Studio.

heartfelt scriptures

Design by Linda Culp Calhoun.

STITCH COUNT (85w x 100h)

14 count	6¹⁄₈" x	7¹⁄₄"
16 count	5³⁄₈" x	6¹⁄₄"
18 count	4³⁄₄" x	5⁵⁄₈"
22 count	3⁷⁄₈" x	4⁵⁄₈"

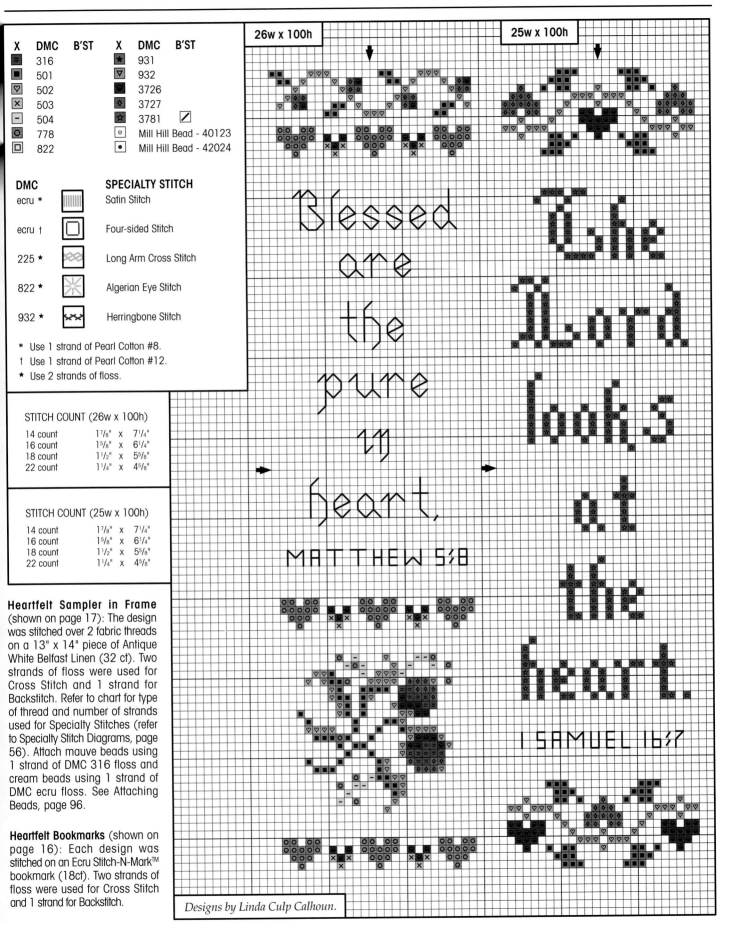

X	DMC	B'ST	X	DMC	B'ST
	316			931	
	501			932	
	502			3726	
	503			3727	
	504			3781	
	778			Mill Hill Bead - 40123	
	822			Mill Hill Bead - 42024	

DMC | | **SPECIALTY STITCH**

ecru * — Satin Stitch

ecru † — Four-sided Stitch

225 * — Long Arm Cross Stitch

822 * — Algerian Eye Stitch

932 * — Herringbone Stitch

* Use 1 strand of Pearl Cotton #8.
† Use 1 strand of Pearl Cotton #12.
★ Use 2 strands of floss.

STITCH COUNT (26w x 100h)

14 count	1⅞"	x	7¼"
16 count	1⅝"	x	6¼"
18 count	1½"	x	5⅝"
22 count	1¼"	x	4⅝"

STITCH COUNT (25w x 100h)

14 count	1⅞"	x	7¼"
16 count	1⅝"	x	6¼"
18 count	1½"	x	5⅝"
22 count	1¼"	x	4⅝"

Heartfelt Sampler in Frame (shown on page 17): The design was stitched over 2 fabric threads on a 13" x 14" piece of Antique White Belfast Linen (32 ct). Two strands of floss were used for Cross Stitch and 1 strand for Backstitch. Refer to chart for type of thread and number of strands used for Specialty Stitches (refer to Specialty Stitch Diagrams, page 56). Attach mauve beads using 1 strand of DMC 316 floss and cream beads using 1 strand of DMC ecru floss. See Attaching Beads, page 96.

Heartfelt Bookmarks (shown on page 16): Each design was stitched on an Ecru Stitch-N-Mark™ bookmark (18ct). Two strands of floss were used for Cross Stitch and 1 strand for Backstitch.

26w x 100h

25w x 100h

Blessed
are
the
pure
in
heart.

MATTHEW 5:8

The
Lord
looks
at
the
heart.

1 SAMUEL 16:7

Designs by Linda Culp Calhoun.

heartfelt scriptures

Heartfelt Sampler in Frame (shown on page 17, chart on pages 54-55): Refer to chart for type of thread and number of strands for Specialty Stitches.

SPECIALITY STITCH DIAGRAMS

(**Note**: Bring threaded needle up at 1 and all odd numbers and down at 2 and all even numbers.)

PULLED STITCHES

When working Pulled Stitches, fabric threads should be pulled tightly together to create an opening in the fabric around the stitch. Figs. show placement of stitch but do not show pulling of the fabric threads. Keep tension even throughout work.

Algerian Eye Stitch: An "eye" is formed in the center of this stitch. Come up at 1, go down in center, and pull tightly toward 3. Come up at 3, go down in center, and pull tightly toward 5; continue working in this manner until stitch is complete (stitches 5-15) (**Fig. 1**). Work row of Algerian Eye Stitches from right to left.

Fig. 1

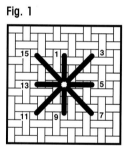

Four-Sided Stitch: This continuous stitch is worked from left to right. Come up at 1 and pull tightly toward 2; then go down at 2 and pull tightly toward 1. Work stitches 3-14 in same manner (**Fig. 2**). Continue working in the same manner to end of row.

Fig. 2

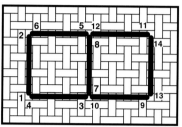

EMBROIDERY STITCHES

Herringbone Stitch: This overlapping stitch is worked continuously from left to right. Complete first stitch (stitches 1-4); then work next stitch (stitches 5-8) as shown in **Fig. 3**. Work all consecutive stitches in the same manner as stitches 5-8.

Fig. 3

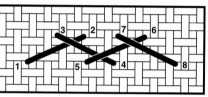

Long Arm Cross Stitch: This overlapping stitch is worked continuously from left to right. Complete first stitch (stitches 1-4); then work next stitch (stitches 5-8) as shown in **Fig. 4**. Work all consecutive stitches in the same manner as stitches 5-8.

Fig. 4

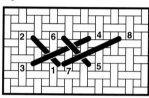

Satin Stitch: This stitch is a series of straight stitches worked side by side (**Fig. 5**). The number of threads worked over and the direction of stitches will vary according to the chart.

Fig. 5

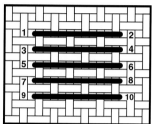

the love of family

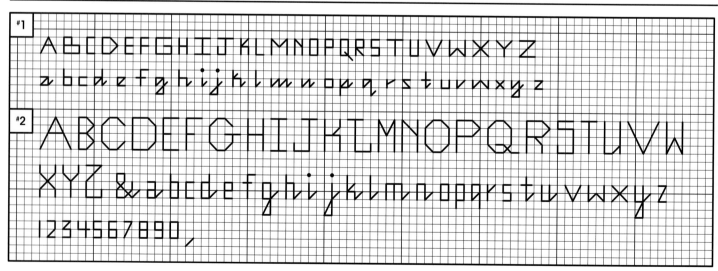

Certificate of Baptism in Frame (shown on page 30, chart on pages 76-77): Using DMC 3781 floss, personalize and date certificate using alphabet #1 for witness names and alphabet and numerals #2 for all other.

FLOWERS OF FAITH

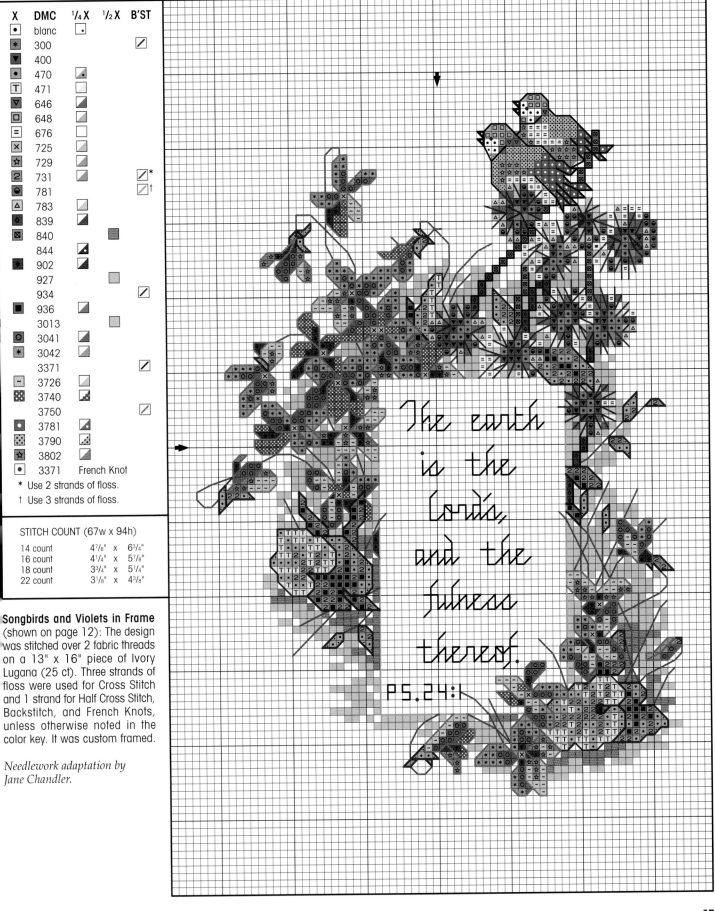

X	DMC	¼ X	½ X	B'ST
·	blanc	·		
✳	300			╱
▼	400			
●	470	◢		
T	471	◢		
◥	646	◢		
▢	648	◢		
=	676	◢		
✕	725	◢		
☆	729	◢		
2	731	◢		╱*
◉	781	◢		╱†
△	783	◢		
◈	839	◢		
⊠	840		▨	
	844	◢		
✴	902	◢		
	927		▨	
	934			╱
■	936	◢		
	3013		▨	
◎	3041	◢		
✳	3042	◢		
	3371			╱
−	3726	◢		
▨	3740	◢		
	3750			╱
◘	3781	◢		
⣿	3790	◢		
☆	3802	◢		
●	3371	French Knot		

* Use 2 strands of floss.
† Use 3 strands of floss.

STITCH COUNT (67w x 94h)

14 count	4⁷⁄₈"	x	6³⁄₄"
16 count	4¼"	x	5⁷⁄₈"
18 count	3³⁄₄"	x	5¼"
22 count	3¹⁄₈"	x	4³⁄₈"

Songbirds and Violets in Frame
(shown on page 12): The design
was stitched over 2 fabric threads
on a 13" x 16" piece of Ivory
Lugana (25 ct). Three strands of
floss were used for Cross Stitch
and 1 strand for Half Cross Stitch,
Backstitch, and French Knots,
unless otherwise noted in the
color key. It was custom framed.

*Needlework adaptation by
Jane Chandler.*

flowers of faith

X	DMC	¼X	B'ST	X	DMC	¼X	B'ST	X	DMC	¼X	½X	B'ST	X	DMC	¼X	B'ST	X	DMC	¼X	B'ST
•	blanc			★	320			2	367			◢*	◉	712			◖	782		
◼	312			▽	322			−	368				△	725				783		
	317				336			✦	420				▽	760				890		

STITCH COUNT (73w x 100h)

14 count	5¼"	x	7¼"	
16 count	4⅝"	x	6¼"	
18 count	4⅛"	x	5⅝"	
22 count	3⅜"	x	4⅝"	

Floral Arbors in Frames (shown on pages 10–11): Each design was stitched over 2 fabric threads on a 14" x 16" piece of Antique White Lugana (25 ct). Three strands of floss were used for Cross Stitch and 1 strand for Half Cross Stitch, Backstitch, and French Knots, unless otherwise noted in the color key. They were custom framed.

X	DMC	¼X	B'ST	X	DMC	
✱	928	◩		◉✱	725	French Knot
	3371	◪	╱	●	3371	French Knot
☒	3755	◱		✱ Use 2 strands of floss.		

Needlework adaptations by Jane Chandler.

59

FLOWERS OF FAITH

STITCH COUNT (80w x 80h)

14 count	5³/₄"	x	5³/₄"
16 count	5"	x	5"
18 count	4¹/₂"	x	4¹/₂"
22 count	3³/₄"	x	3³/₄"

God is Love

X	DMC	B'ST	X	DMC	B'ST	X	DMC	B'ST
>	316		★	930		✕	3727	
	433	✓	⊠	931		■	3740	✓
2	580		C	932			3750	✓
V	581			934	✓	◉	3802	
▢	742		■	936		●	3822	
✲	833		✦	3041		✚	3823	
−	834	✓	H	3042		●	3740	French Knot
■	902	✓	⊠	3726				

Pansy Bouquet Pillow (shown on page 13): The design was stitched over 2 fabric threads on a 15" square of Ivory Lugana (25 ct). Three strands of floss were used for Cross Stitch and 1 strand for Backstitch and French Knots.

Centering design, trim stitched piece to measure 10" square. To complete pillow, see Finishing Instructions, page 61.

Needlework adaptation by Jane Chandler.

X	DMC	¼X	B'ST	X	DMC	¼X	B'ST
•	blanc	•		○	676		
−	ecru			□	726		
▽	402	◢		▦	732	◪	
★	434	◢			890		◸
2	580	◢		■	976	◢	
▽	610	◢	◸	◇	3013	◢	
▣	644	◢		T	3362	◢	
	647		◸				

STITCH COUNT (40w x 71h)

14 count	2⅞"	x	5⅛"
16 count	2½"	x	4½"
18 count	2¼"	x	4"
22 count	1⅞"	x	3¼"

Daisy Pillow (shown on page 13): The design was stitched over 2 fabric threads on an 11" x 20" piece of Ivory Lugana (25 ct). Three strands of floss were used for Cross Stitch and 1 strand for Backstitch.

For pillow, you will need a 5" x 16" piece of lightweight fabric for lining, 2" x 34" bias fabric strip for cording, 34" length of ¼" dia. purchased cord, two 13" x 10½" pieces of fabric for pillow front and back, and polyester fiberfill.

Centering design, trim stitched piece to measure 5" x 16".

For band, matching right sides and short edges, fold stitched piece in half. Using a ½" seam allowance, sew short edges together. Turn band right side out. Repeat for band lining.

Center cord on wrong side of bias strip; matching long edges, fold strip over cord. Use a zipper foot to baste along length of strip close to cord; trim seam allowance to ½" and cut length of cording in half. Matching raw edges, pin one length of cording to right side of one edge of band. Ends of cording should overlap approximately 2"; pin overlapping end out of way. Starting 2" from beginning end of cording and ending 4" from overlapping end, baste cording to band. On overlapping end of cording, remove 2½" of basting; fold end of fabric back and trim cord so that it meets beginning end of cord. Fold end of fabric ½" to wrong side; wrap fabric over beginning end of cording. Finish basting cording to band. Repeat for remaining length of cording and edge of band. Matching right sides and seam and leaving an opening for turning, use a ½" seam allowance to sew band and lining together at edges. Turn band right side out and blind stitch opening closed.

For pillow, match right sides and raw edges of pillow front and back. Leaving an opening for turning, use a ½" seam allowance to sew fabric pieces together; trim seam allowances diagonally at corners. Turn pillow right side out, carefully pushing corners outward; stuff pillow lightly with polyester fiberfill and blind stitch opening closed.

Referring to photo, place band around pillow.

Needlework adaptation by Jane Chandler.

FINISHING INSTRUCTONS

Pansy Bouquet Pillow (shown on page 13, chart on page 60): For pillow, you will need 10" square piece of fabric for backing, 6" x 72" fabric strip for ruffle (pieced as necessary), and polyester fiberfill.

For ruffle, press short edges of fabric strip ½" to wrong side. Matching wrong sides and long edges, fold strip in half; press. Machine baste ½" from raw edges; gather fabric strip to fit stitched piece. Matching raw edges, pin ruffle to right side of stitched piece, overlapping short ends ¼". Use a ½" seam allowance to sew ruffle to stitched piece.

Matching right sides and leaving an opening for turning, use a ½" seam allowance to sew stitched piece and backing fabric together. Trim seam allowances diagonally at corners; turn pillow right side out, carefully pushing corners outward. Stuff pillow with polyester fiberfill and blind stitch opening closed.

AMAZING GRACE

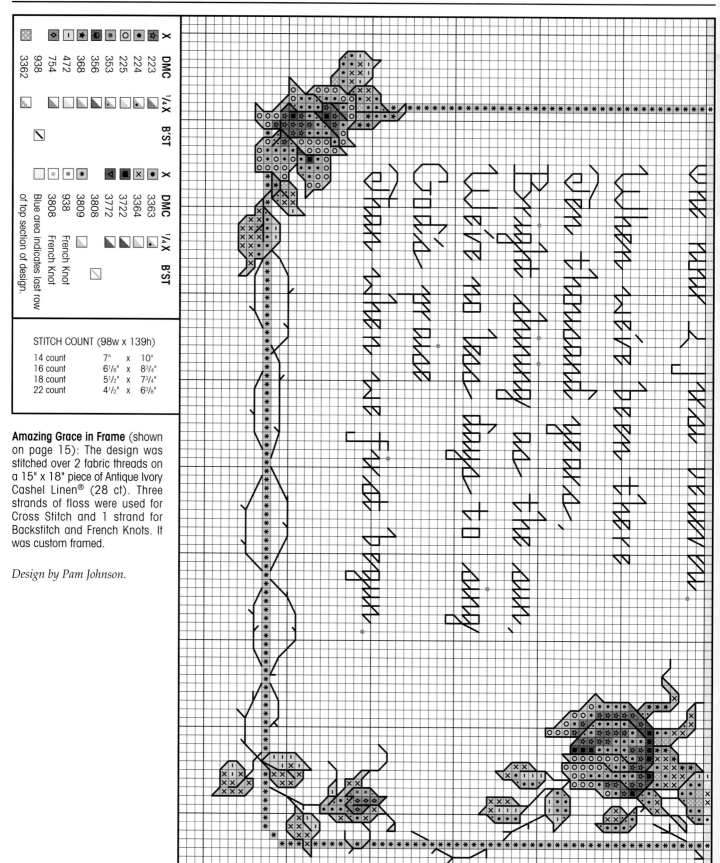

X									DMC	¼X	B'ST
									223		
									224		
									225		
									353		
									356		
									368		
									472		
									754		
									938		
									3362		

X						DMC	¼X	B'ST
						3363		
						3364		
						3722		
						3772		
						3808		
						3808		
						3809		
						938	French Knot	
						3808	French Knot	

Blue area indicates last row
of top section of design.

STITCH COUNT (98w x 139h)

14 count	7"	x	10"
16 count	6⅛"	x	8¾"
18 count	5½"	x	7¾"
22 count	4½"	x	6⅜"

Amazing Grace in Frame (shown on page 15): The design was stitched over 2 fabric threads on a 15" x 18" piece of Antique Ivory Cashel Linen® (28 ct). Three strands of floss were used for Cross Stitch and 1 strand for Backstitch and French Knots. It was custom framed.

Design by Pam Johnson.

HERB GARDEN

X	DMC	¼X	B'ST	X	DMC	¼X	B'ST
•	blanc			H	3348		
▨	319	◪	◹	◇	3354		
▧	320	◪		◉	3687		
▼	367	◪		═	3688		
◉	368	◪		▲	3740		
2	822			✕	3752		
★	931			◎	3790	◪	
◻	932			△	3821		
	3031		◹	+	3822		
⊟	3041			●	3031	French Knot	
▬	3042			◻	Blue area indicates		
♥	3347	◪			first row of right section		
					of design.		

Herb Sampler in Frame (shown on page 19): The design was stitched over 2 fabric threads on a 17" x 16" piece of Light Sand Cashel Linen® (28 ct). Three strands of floss were used for Cross Stitch and 1 strand for Backstitch and French Knots. It was custom framed.

Garden Towel (shown on page 21): The sage, thyme, and oregano from the Herb Sampler (refer to photo) were stitched on the Aida (14 ct) border of an Ecru Velour Fingertip™ towel. Three strands of floss were used for Cross Stitch and 1 strand for Backstitch.

Parsley and Basil Plant Pokes (shown on page 21): The parsley and basil from the Herb Sampler (refer to photo) were each stitched on a 6" square of Ivory Aida (11 ct). Four strands of floss were used for Cross Stitch and 1 strand for Backstitch and French Knot.

For each plant poke, you will need a 6" square piece of lightweight cream fabric for backing, craft stick, clear-drying craft glue, fabric stiffener, and small foam brush.

Apply a heavy coat of fabric stiffener to wrong side of stitched piece using small foam brush. Matching wrong sides, place stitched piece on backing fabric, smoothing stitched piece while pressing fabric pieces together; allow to dry. Apply fabric stiffener to backing fabric; allow to dry. Cut out close to edges of stitched design. Refer to photo to glue craft stick to back of each stitched piece.

Herb Bookmark (shown on page 21): The basil, chives, dill, rosemary, and mint from the Herb Sampler (refer to photo) were stitched on an Ecru Stitch-N-Mark™ bookmark (18 ct). Two strands of floss were used for Cross Stitch and 1 strand for Backstitch and French Knots.

Design by Deborah Lambein.

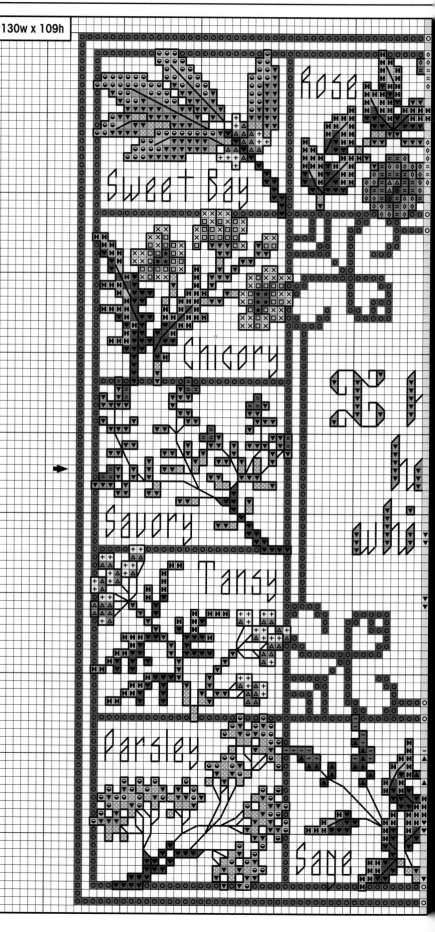

130w x 109h

herb garden

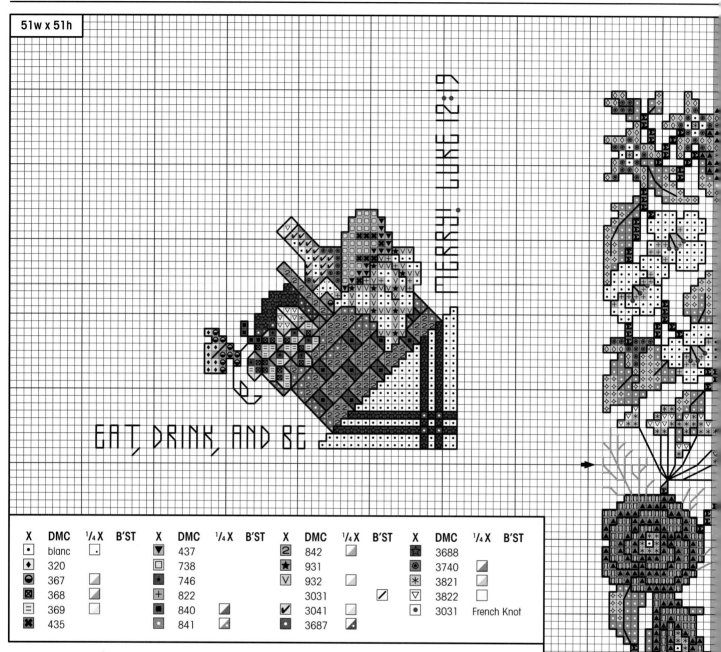

X	DMC	¼ X	B'ST	X	DMC	¼ X	B'ST	X	DMC	¼ X	B'ST	X	DMC	¼ X	B'ST
•	blanc	•		▼	437			2	842			★	3688		
◆	320			□	738			★	931			◉	3740		
◖	367			●	746			V	932			✳	3821		
⊠	368			+	822				3031		/	▽	3822		
=	369			■	840			✔	3041			•	3031	French Knot	
✖	435			●	841			●	3687						

"Be Merry" Bread Cloth (shown on page 21): The design was stitched on one corner of an Ivory Breadcover (14 ct) with design 7 fabric threads from beginning of fringe. Three strands of floss were used for Cross Stitch and 1 strand for Backstitch and French Knots.

Design by Deborah Lambein.

Beehive Jar Lid (shown on page 21): The bees and beehive from the Garden Sampler (refer to photo) were stitched on a 6" square of Light Sand Cashel Linen® (28 ct). Three strands of floss were used for Cross Stitch and 1 strand for Backstitch.

For jar lid, you will need a wide-mouth jar lid, 3¼" dia. circle of adhesive mounting board, 3¼" dia. circle of batting, and clear-drying craft glue.

Centering design, trim stitched piece to a 5¼" dia. circle.

Remove paper from adhesive mounting board; center batting on adhesive board and press in place. With right side facing up, center stitched piece on batting. Fold edges of stitched piece to back of adhesive board; glue fabric edges to back of adhesive board. Glue stitched piece inside jar lid.

X	DMC	¼X	B'ST
•	blanc		
Σ	319	◩	◩
▫	367		
✧	368		
2	642		
▢	676		
8	680	◩	
⊓	729	◩	◩
✚	822		
▪	931		
▽	932		
◉	3031	◩	◩
◎	3041		
◇	3042		
▲	3687		
⊓	3688		
2	3752		
◓	3790		
✳	3821	◩	
▽	3822		
●	3031	French Knot	
▨	Grey area indicates first		
	row of right section		
	of design.		

STITCH COUNT (85w x 100h)

14 count	6⅛"	x	7¼"
16 count	5⅜"	x	6¼"
18 count	4¾"	x	5⅝"
22 count	3⅞"	x	4⅝"

Garden Sampler in Frame (shown on page 20): The design was stitched over 2 fabric threads on a 14" x 15" piece of Light Sand Cashel Linen® (28 ct). Three strands of floss were used for Cross Stitch and 1 strand for Backstitch and French Knots. It was custom framed.

Design by Deborah Lambein.

The 23rd Psalm

X	DMC	¼X	B'ST
	blanc		
	315		
	316		
	433		
	435		
	535		
	647		
	744		
	778		
	931		

X	DMC	¼X	½X	B'ST
	938			
	945			
	3024			
	3051			
	3364			
	3726			
	3750			
	3761			
	3766			
	3770			

X	DMC	¼X	B'ST
	3773		
	3823		
	3826		
	Kreinik Very Fine Braid - 002		
	315 French Knot		
	315 * French Knot		
	931 French Knot		
	3750 French Knot		

X	DMC	¼X	B'ST
	Kreinik Very Fine Braid - 002		
	French Knot		

Blue area indicates last row of top section of design.

* Use 3 strands of floss.

STITCH COUNT (102w x 140h)

14 count	7³/₈"	x	10"
16 count	6³/₈"	x	8³/₄"
18 count	5³/₄"	x	7⁷/₈"
22 count	4³/₄"	x	6³/₈"

The 23rd Psalm in Frame (shown on page 23): The design was stitched over 2 fabric threads on a 15" x 18" piece of Antique Ivory Cashel Linen® (28 ct). Three strands of floss or 1 strand of Braid were used for Cross Stitch, 2 strands for Half Cross Stitch and 1 strand for Backstitch and French Knots, unless otherwise noted in the color key. It was custom framed.

Design by Sandy Orton of Kooler Design Studio.

GUARDIAN ANGEL

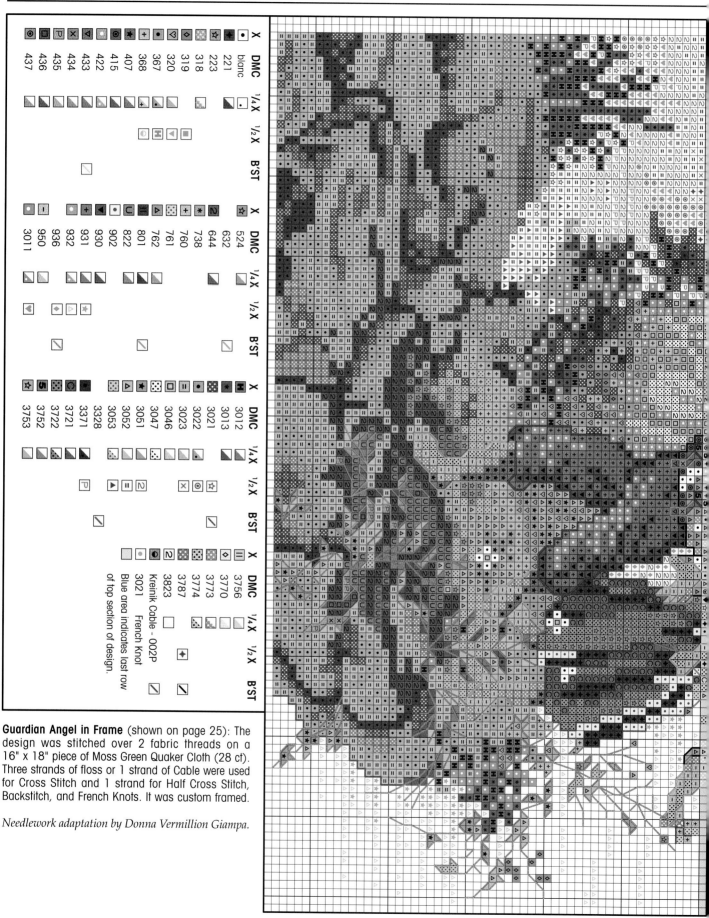

X	DMC
⊙	437
◩	436
P	435
✕	434
◪	433
◭	422
◒	415
⊚	407
✦	368
+	367
◦	320
◁	319
◈	318
▨	223
✩	221
✹	blanc

X	DMC
◦	524
Ⅰ	632
◉	644
+	738
◀	760
•	761
C	762
▣	801
▶	822
⊡	902
+	930
✱	931
2	932
	936
✩	950
	3011

X	DMC
✩	3012
5	3013
⊙	3021
■	3022
◨	3023
◇	3046
★	3047
⊡	3051
◻	3052
▨	3053
✱	3328
✳	3371
H	3721
	3722
	3752
	3753

X	DMC
▢	3756
◦	3770
◑	3773
2	3774
✕	3787
⊙	3823
✩	Kreinik Cable - 002P
◆	3021 French Knot

Blue area indicates last row of top section of design.

Guardian Angel in Frame (shown on page 25): The design was stitched over 2 fabric threads on a 16" x 18" piece of Moss Green Quaker Cloth (28 ct). Three strands of floss or 1 strand of Cable were used for Cross Stitch and 1 strand for Half Cross Stitch, Backstitch, and French Knots. It was custom framed.

Needlework adaptation by Donna Vermillion Giampa.

the love of family

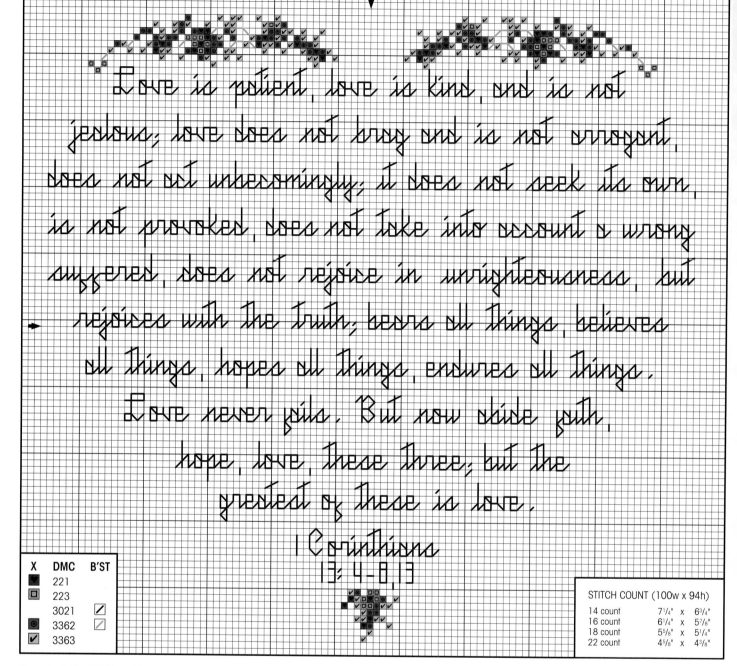

Love is patient, love is kind, and is not jealous; love does not brag and is not arrogant, does not act unbecomingly; it does not seek its own, is not provoked, does not take into account a wrong suffered, does not rejoice in unrighteousness, but rejoices with the truth; bears all things, believes all things, hopes all things, endures all things. Love never fails. But now abide faith, hope, love, these three; but the greatest of these is love.

1 Corinthians 13:4-8, 13

X	DMC	B'ST
■	221	
□	223	
	3021	╱
◉	3362	╱
✔	3363	

STITCH COUNT (100w x 94h)

14 count	7¼"	x	6¾"
16 count	6¼"	x	5⅞"
18 count	5⅝"	x	5¼"
22 count	4⅝"	x	4⅜"

"Love Is Patient" Pillow (shown on page 26): The design was stitched over 2 fabric threads on a 15" square of Cream Quaker Cloth (28 ct). Three strands of floss were used for Cross Stitch and 1 strand for Backstitch.

For pillow, you will need a 15" square of fabric for pillow backing, 30" length of ¼" dia. purchased cording with attached seam allowance, 53" length of 2"w flat lace, and polyester fiberfill.

For pillow front, refer to photo and trim stitched piece approximately 1¼" from design on all sides. Cut backing fabric same size as pillow front.

If needed, trim seam allowance of cording to ½"; pin cording to right side of pillow front, making a ⅜" clip in seam allowance of cording as needed at curves and points. Ends of cording should overlap approximately 4". Turn overlapped ends of cording toward outside edge of pillow front; baste cording to pillow front.

Press short ends of lace ½" to wrong side; machine baste ¼" from straight edge and gather lace to fit pillow front. Matching gathered edge of lace with raw edges of pillow front and beginning at bottom edge, pin lace to right side of pillow front; machine baste through all layers. Blind stitch pressed edges of lace together.

Matching right sides, raw edges, and leaving an opening for turning, use a ½" seam allowance to sew pillow front and pillow back together. Trim seam allowances and clip curves as needed; turn pillow right side out. Stuff pillow with polyester fiberfill and blind stitch opening closed.

Design by Linda Culp Calhoun.

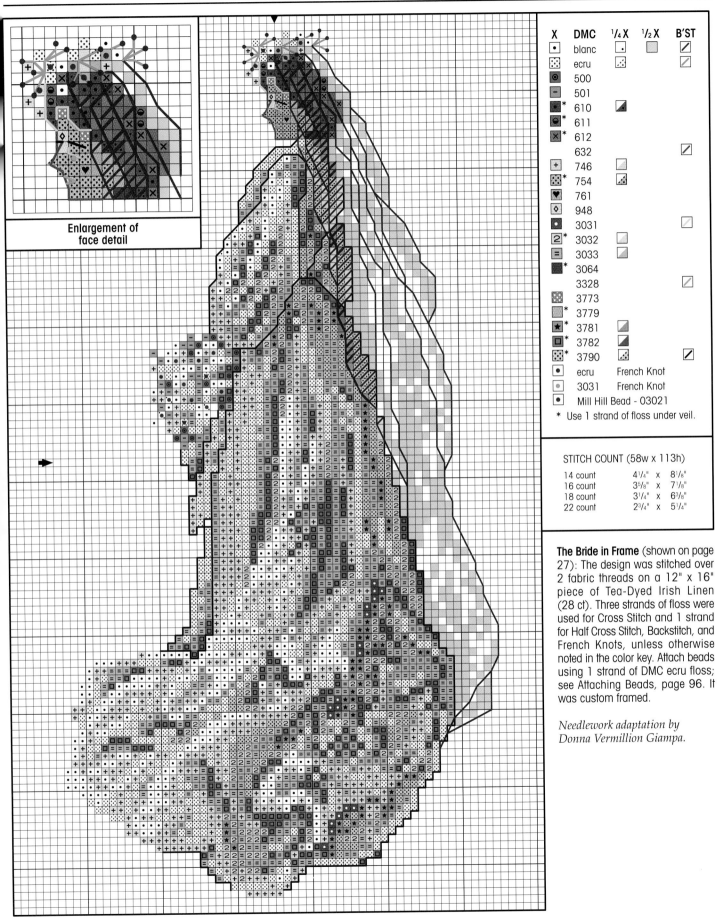

Enlargement of face detail

X	DMC	¼ X	½ X	B'ST
•	blanc	•	▨	╱
⊠	ecru	⊠		╱
◉	500			
—	501			
✶ *	610	◺		
◉ *	611			
⊠ *	612			
	632			╱
+	746	◹		
▨ *	754	◹		
♥	761			
◇	948			
◘	3031			╱
2 *	3032	◹		
=	3033	◺		
■ *	3064			
	3328			╱
▨	3773			
▨ *	3779			
★ *	3781	◺		
▢ *	3782	◺		
▨ *	3790	◹		╱
◉	ecru	French Knot		
◉	3031	French Knot		
◉	Mill Hill Bead - 03021			
* Use 1 strand of floss under veil.				

STITCH COUNT (58w x 113h)

14 count	4¼"	x	8⅛"	
16 count	3⅝"	x	7⅛"	
18 count	3¼"	x	6⅜"	
22 count	2¾"	x	5¼"	

The Bride in Frame (shown on page 27): The design was stitched over 2 fabric threads on a 12" x 16" piece of Tea-Dyed Irish Linen (28 ct). Three strands of floss were used for Cross Stitch and 1 strand for Half Cross Stitch, Backstitch, and French Knots, unless otherwise noted in the color key. Attach beads using 1 strand of DMC ecru floss; see Attaching Beads, page 96. It was custom framed.

Needlework adaptation by Donna Vermillion Giampa.

center name

center name

center date

STITCH COUNT (47w x 77h)

14 count	3³/₈"	x 5¹/₂"
16 count	3"	x 4⁷/₈"
18 count	2⁵/₈"	x 4³/₈"
22 count	2¹/₄"	x 3¹/₂"

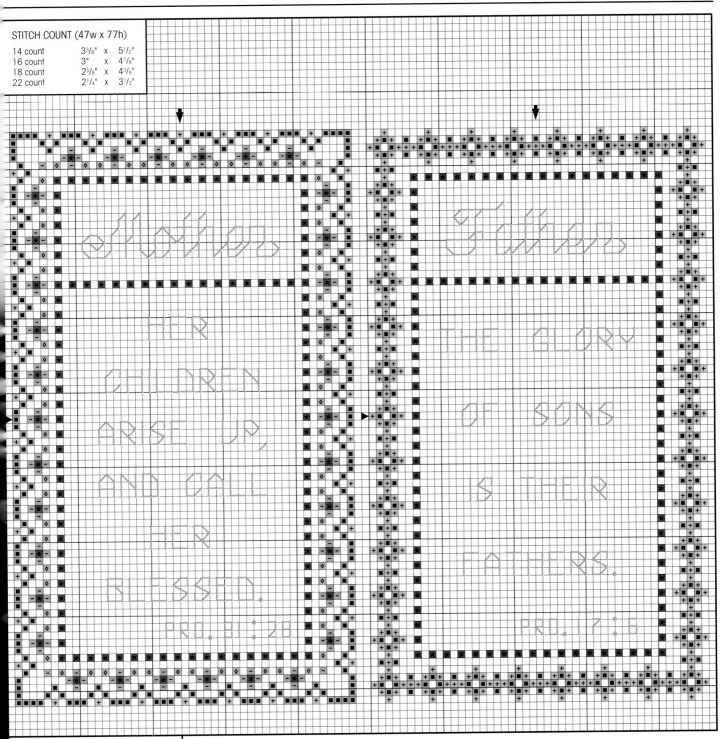

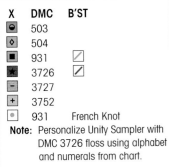

X	DMC	B'ST	
⊖	503		
◇	504		
■	931	/	
✱	3726	/	
–	3727		
+	3752		
⊙	931		French Knot

Note: Personalize Unity Sampler with DMC 3726 floss using alphabet and numerals from chart.

Unity Sampler in Frame (shown on page 28): The design was stitched over 2 fabric threads on a 14" x 15" piece of Antique White Cashel Linen® (28 ct). Three strands of floss were used for Cross Stitch and 1 strand for Backstitch and French Knots. It was custom framed.

Mother and Father Samplers in Frames (shown on page 29): Each design was stitched over 2 fabric threads on an 11" x 14" piece of Antique White Cashel Linen® (28 ct). Three strands of floss were used for Cross Stitch and 1 strand for Backstitch and French Knots. They were custom framed.

Designs by Mary Scott.

75

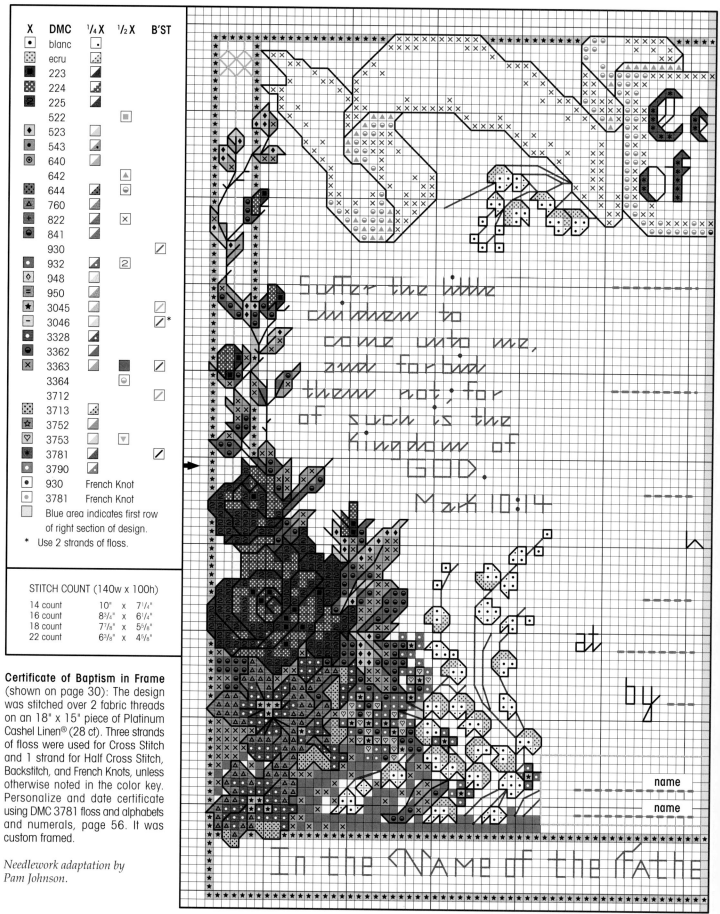

X	DMC	¼ X	½ X	B'ST
•	blanc	•		
	ecru			
■	223			
	224			
	225			
	522		■	
◆	523			
•	543			
⊙	640			
	642		▲	
	644		⊖	
△	760			
+	822		✕	
	841			
	930			╱
•	932		2	
◇	948			
=	950			
★	3045			╱
−	3046			╱ *
	3328			
⊙	3362			
✕	3363		■	╱
	3364		⊖	
	3712			╱
	3713			
☆	3752			
♡	3753		▽	
✳	3781			╱
•	3790			
•	930	French Knot		
•	3781	French Knot		
▢		Blue area indicates first row of right section of design.		

* Use 2 strands of floss.

STITCH COUNT (140w x 100h)

14 count	10"	x	7¼"
16 count	8¾"	x	6¼"
18 count	7⅞"	x	5⅝"
22 count	6⅜"	x	4⅝"

Certificate of Baptism in Frame (shown on page 30): The design was stitched over 2 fabric threads on an 18" x 15" piece of Platinum Cashel Linen® (28 ct). Three strands of floss were used for Cross Stitch and 1 strand for Half Cross Stitch, Backstitch, and French Knots, unless otherwise noted in the color key. Personalize and date certificate using DMC 3781 floss and alphabets and numerals, page 56. It was custom framed.

Needlework adaptation by Pam Johnson.

center name

child of

center names

born on

center date

as baptized

center date

center name

center name

Witnesses

name

name

r, of the Son, and of the Holy Ghost.

the love of family

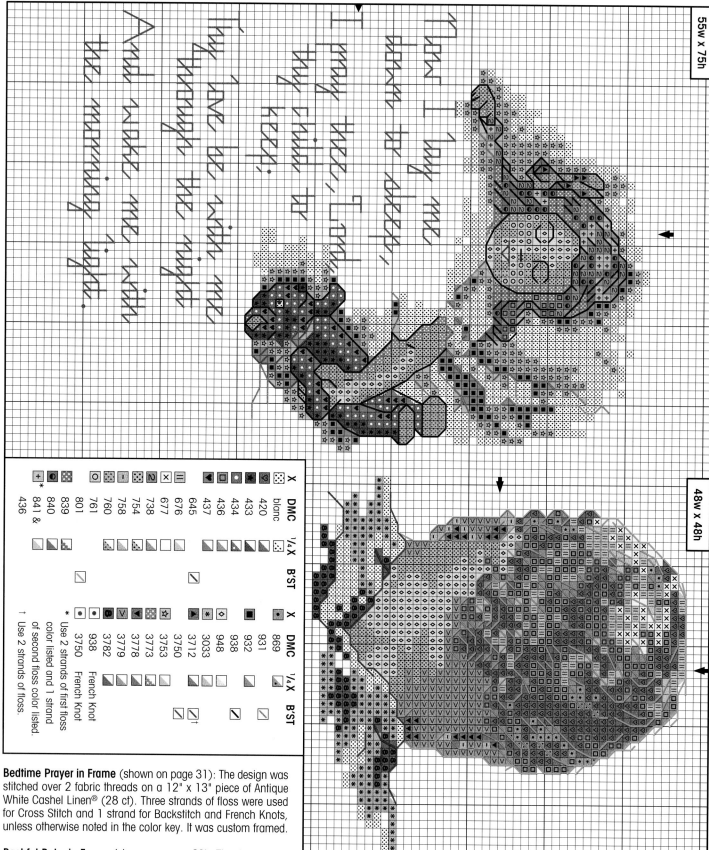

Bedtime Prayer in Frame (shown on page 31): The design was stitched over 2 fabric threads on a 12" x 13" piece of Antique White Cashel Linen® (28 ct). Three strands of floss were used for Cross Stitch and 1 strand for Backstitch and French Knots, unless otherwise noted in the color key. It was custom framed.

Bashful Baby in Frame (shown on page 31): The design was stitched over 2 fabric threads on a 12" square of Antique White Cashel Linen® (28 ct). Three strands of floss were used for Cross Stitch and 1 strand for Backstitch. It was custom framed.

Needlework adaptations by Pam Johnson.

Lady Liberty

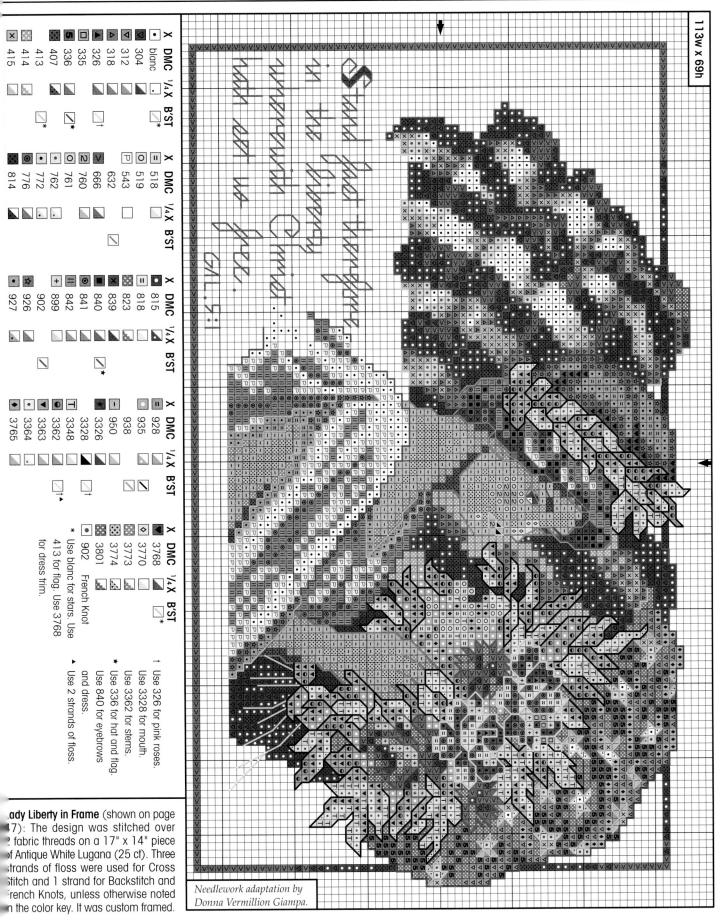

X					¼X	B'ST	DMC
⊠	⊠				·		blanc
⊠	⊠						304
▣			▶				312
◩	◩	◩	◩	◩		◪	318
						◪*	326
							335
						◪†	336
					□↑		407
							413
						◪*	414
							415

X			¼X	B'ST	DMC
▨	⊡	·	◫	◪	518
	○	·			519
	▣P				543
	○				632
	②				666
	○				760
	·		□		761
				◪*	762
					772
					776
					814

X								¼X	B'ST	DMC
⊡	☆	⊞	●	⊡	▦	⊞	◫		◪	815
	+	▥	⊡	■	▦	=				818
									◪*	823
										839
										840
										841
										842
										899
										902
										926
										927

X							¼X	B'ST	DMC
◆	·	◀	◐	▣	⊤	▣			928
				⊤		◫			935
									938
									950
							◪		3326
									3328
								◪*	3348
									3362
									3363
									3364
									3365

X			¼X	B'ST	DMC	
◩	⊡	⊠	◫	◪	3768	
	◇	◪		◪*	3770	
					3773	
					3774	
					3801	
◩	●				902	French Knot

† Use 326 for pink roses.
Use 3328 for mouth.
Use 3362 for stems.
★ Use 336 for hat and flag.
Use 840 for eyebrows and dress.
▲ Use 2 strands of floss.
* Use blanc for stars. Use 413 for flag. Use 3768 for dress trim.

Lady Liberty in Frame (shown on page 47): The design was stitched over 2 fabric threads on a 17" x 14" piece of Antique White Lugana (25 ct). Three strands of floss were used for Cross Stitch and 1 strand for Backstitch and French Knots, unless otherwise noted in the color key. It was custom framed.

Needlework adaptation by Donna Vermillion Giampa.

children of god

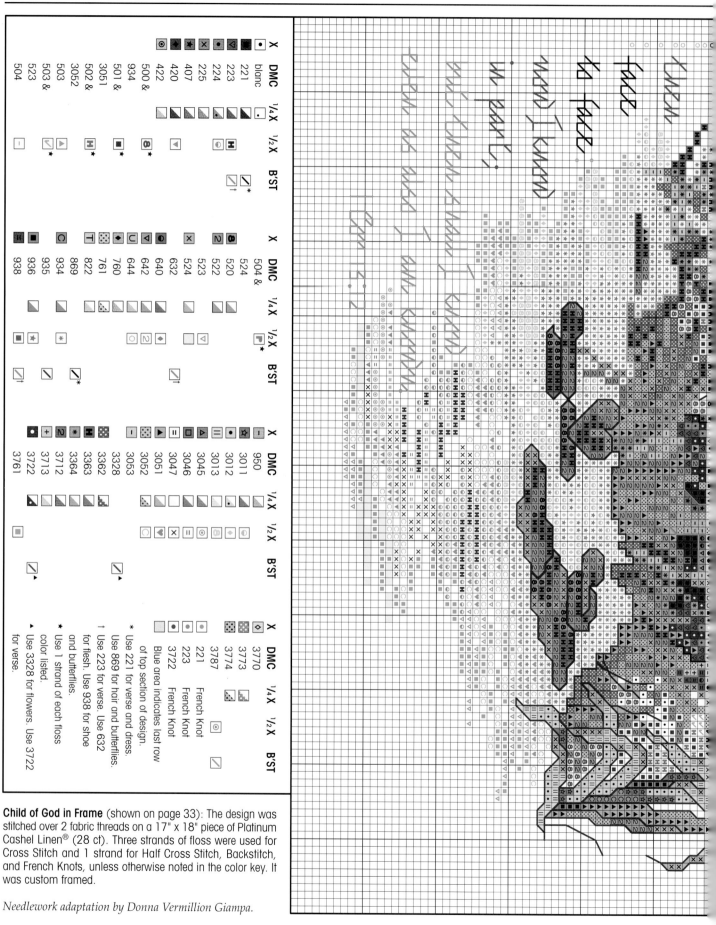

The color key (read vertically):

X	¼X	½X	B'ST	DMC
				blanc
				221
				223
				224
				225
				407
				420
				422
				500 &
				501 &
				502 &
				3051
				3052
				503
				503 &
				523
				523
				504
				504

X	¼X	½X	B'ST	DMC
				504 &
				520
				522
				523
				524
				632
				640
				642
				644
				760
				761
				822
				869
				934
				935
				936
				938

X	¼X	½X	B'ST	DMC
				950
				3011
				3012
				3013
				3045
				3046
				3047
				3051
				3052
				3053
				3328
				3362
				3363
				3364
				3712
				3713
				3722
				3761

X	¼X	½X	B'ST	DMC
				3770
				3773
				3774
				3787
				221 French Knot
				223 French Knot
				3722 French Knot

* Use 221 for verse and dress. Use 869 for hair and butterflies.
† Use 223 for verse. Use 938 for shoe and butterflies.
for flesh. Use 632 for verse.
Blue area indicates last row of top section of design.
★ Use 1 strand of each floss color listed.
► Use 3328 for flowers. Use 3722 for verse.

Child of God in Frame (shown on page 33): The design was stitched over 2 fabric threads on a 17" x 18" piece of Platinum Cashel Linen® (28 ct). Three strands of floss were used for Cross Stitch and 1 strand for Half Cross Stitch, Backstitch, and French Knots, unless otherwise noted in the color key. It was custom framed.

Needlework adaptation by Donna Vermillion Giampa.

STITCH COUNT (116w x 139h)

14 count	8³/₈"	x	10"
16 count	7¹/₄"	x	8³/₄"
18 count	6¹/₂"	x	7³/₄"
22 count	5³/₈"	x	6³/₈"

children of god

X	DMC	¼ X	½ X	B'ST
•	blanc			∕*
	221			∕†
*	223			
□	224			
	310			∕†
X	318		⊙	∕
▲	413			
●	414			
	415		★	
	420			
■	433			
	435			
O	436			
−	437			
⊠	502			
	597			
●	598			
	632			∕*
*	640			
▼	642			
O	644			
	727			
	760			
X	761			
2	762			
♥	782			
☆	783			
☆	822			
T	839			
C	840			
	841			
U	842			
★	869			∕
	938			∕
+	950			
8	3021			
T	3045			
•	3046			
‖	3047			
■	3064			
8	3078			
	3328			∕
⊖	3362			
▽	3363			
+	3364			
■	3712			
−	3713			
⊙	3722			
=	3753			
◇	3770			
	3773			
	3774			
‖	3787			
■	3808			∕
O	3809			
▲	3810			
−	3811			
	3820			
H	3822			

X	DMC		X	DMC	
⊙	221	French Knot	⊙	3808	French Knot
⊙	413	French Knot			
●	781	French Knot			
⊙	938	French Knot			

* Use 632 for flesh and hair. For Design #2, use blanc for slate.

† For Design #1, use 310 for shoes and stockings. Use 221 for all other.

STITCH COUNT (74w x 102h)		STITCH COUNT (85w x 96h)	
14 count	5³⁄₈" x 7³⁄₈"	14 count	6¹⁄₈" x 6⁷⁄₈"
16 count	4⁵⁄₈" x 6³⁄₈"	16 count	5³⁄₈" x 6"
18 count	4¹⁄₈" x 5³⁄₄"	18 count	4³⁄₄" x 5³⁄₈"
22 count	3³⁄₈" x 4³⁄₄"	22 count	3⁷⁄₈" x 4³⁄₈"

Washday in Frame (shown on page 35) and **Little Scholars in Frame** (shown on page 34): Each design was stitched over 2 fabric threads on a 14" x 15" piece of Cream Cashel Linen® (28 ct). Three strands of floss were used for Cross Stitch and 1 strand for Half Cross Stitch, Backstitch, and French Knots. They were custom framed.

Needlework adaptations by Donna Vermillion Giampa.

MY PRAYER

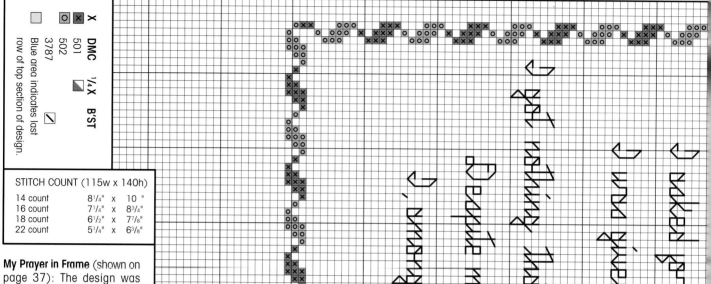

STITCH COUNT (115w x 140h)

14 count	8 1/4"	x	10 "
16 count	7 1/4"	x	8 3/4"
18 count	6 1/2"	x	7 7/8"
22 count	5 1/4"	x	6 3/8"

My Prayer in Frame (shown on page 37): The design was stitched over 2 fabric threads on a 16" x 18" piece of Light Mocha Cashel Linen® (28 ct). Three strands of floss were used for Cross Stitch and 1 strand for Backstitch. It was custom framed.

*Design by
Linda Culp Calhoun.*

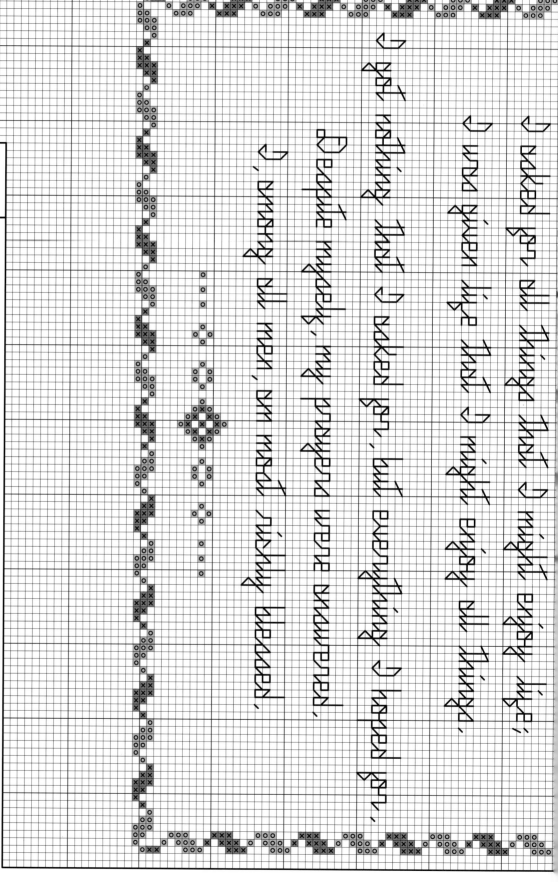

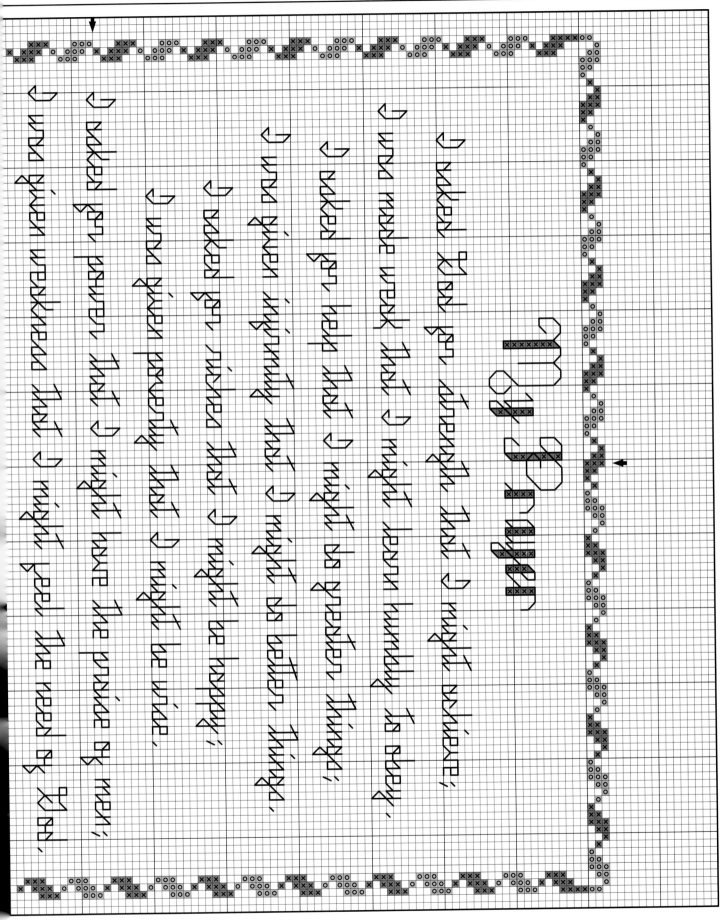

NOAH'S ARK

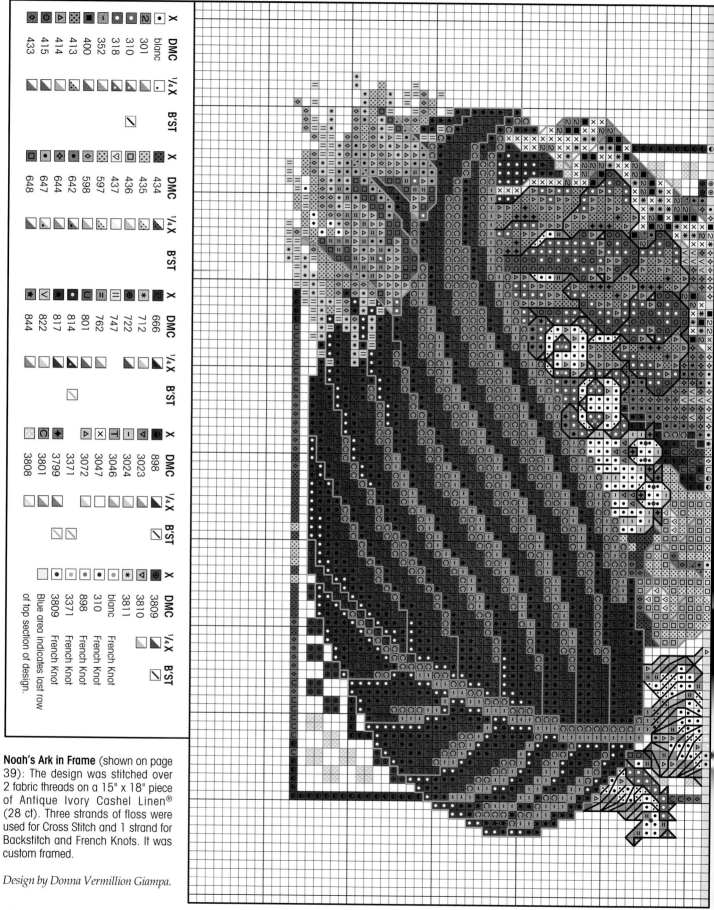

X										DMC	1/4X	B'ST
◆	◎	■	▶	▨	■	1	⊞	2	·	blanc		
										301		
										310		
										318		◥
										352		
										400		
										413		
										414		
										415		
										433		

X										DMC	1/4X	B'ST
▣	·	◆	◇	⊡	☑	□	⊡	▨		434		
										435		
										436		
										437		
										597		
										598		
										642		
										644		
										647		
										648		

X										DMC	1/4X	B'ST
★	☑	■	●	C	⊟	⊟	⊕	✳	▨	666		
										712		
										722		
										747		
										762		
										801		
										814		
										817		◪
										822		
										844		

X							DMC	1/4X	B'ST
▨	◔	◆	▶	✕	⊟	◀	898		
							3023		
							3024		
							3046		
							3047		
							3072		
							3371		◪
							3799		
							3801		
							3808		

X						DMC	1/4X	B'ST
□	·	▨	✳	◀	◉	3809		◪
						3810		
						3811		
						blanc	French Knot
						310	French Knot
						898	French Knot
						3371	French Knot
						3809	French Knot

Blue area indicates last row of top section of design.

Noah's Ark in Frame (shown on page 39): The design was stitched over 2 fabric threads on a 15" x 18" piece of Antique Ivory Cashel Linen® (28 ct). Three strands of floss were used for Cross Stitch and 1 strand for Backstitch and French Knots. It was custom framed.

Design by Donna Vermillion Giampa.

STITCH COUNT (89w x 128h)

14 count	6³/₈"	x	9¹/₄"
16 count	5⁵/₈"	x	8"
18 count	5"	x	7¹/₈"
22 count	4¹/₈"	x	5⁷/₈"

ABUNDANT THANKSGIVING

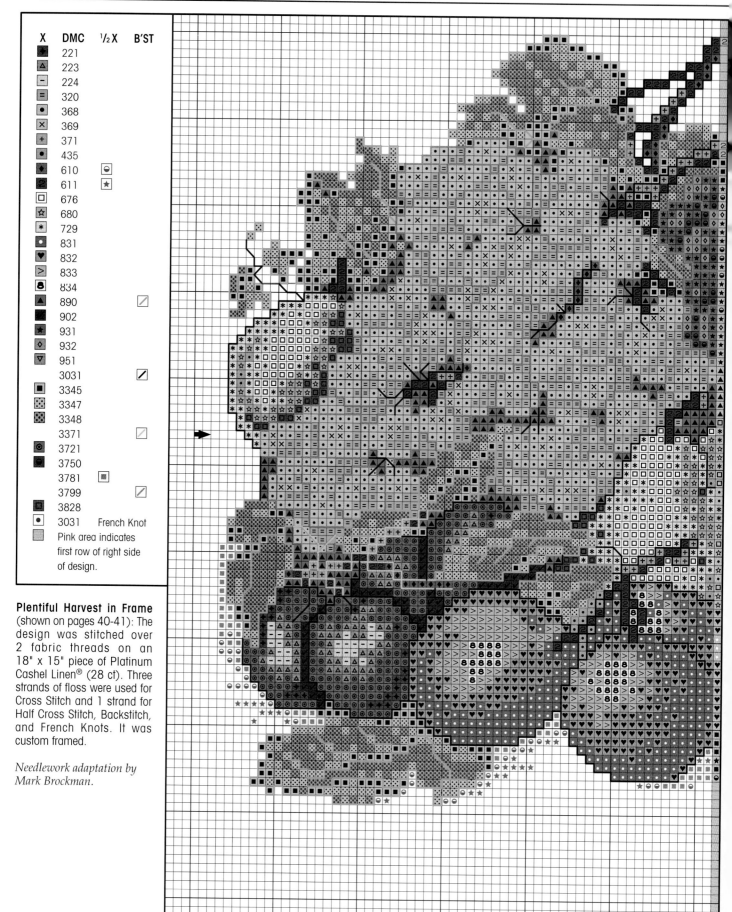

X	DMC	½ X	B'ST
★	221		
▲	223		
−	224		
=	320		
●	368		
×	369		
+	371		
●	435		
◆	610	⊖	
2	611	★	
□	676		
☆	680		
✳	729		
◐	831		
♥	832		
>	833		
8	834		
▲	890		╱
■	902		
★	931		
◇	932		
▽	951		
	3031		╱
■	3345		
▓	3347		
▒	3348		
	3371		╱
◉	3721		
●	3750		
	3781	■	
	3799		╱
■	3828		
●	3031	French Knot	
	Pink area indicates first row of right side of design.		

Plentiful Harvest in Frame
(shown on pages 40-41): The design was stitched over 2 fabric threads on an 18" x 15" piece of Platinum Cashel Linen® (28 ct). Three strands of floss were used for Cross Stitch and 1 strand for Half Cross Stitch, Backstitch, and French Knots. It was custom framed.

Needlework adaptation by Mark Brockman.

90w x 90h

We plough we sow the open fields All blest each one its harvest yields. And unto him our thanks we give Who blesses so that we may live.

X	DMC	¼ X	B'ST	X	DMC	¼ X	B'ST	X	DMC	¼ X
	336		╱	+	677			◆	3345	◢
=	341	◢		●	680	◢		▢	3346	◢
	433		╱	☆	729	◢		U	3347	◢
	610		╱*	-	772			♡	3348	◢
◉	611	◢		▨	792	◢	╱	○	3747	◢
✳	612	◢			793	◢		★	3807	◢
▲	613	◢			794	◢		●	792	French Knot
▢	676				935			╱	* Use 2 strands of floss.	

Blessed Harvest in Frame (shown on page 42): The design was stitched over 2 fabric threads on a 15" square of Platinum Cashel Linen® (28 ct). Three strands of floss were used for Cross Stitch and 1 strand for Backstitch and French Knots, unless otherwise noted in the color key. It was custom framed.

Needlework adaptation by Donna Vermillion Giampa.

X	DMC	¼ X	½ X	B'ST
•	blanc	•		
◆	221	◺		
▣	223	◺		
◍	224	◺		
⊠	225	◺		
▦	407	◪		
	420		▩	
▣	433	◺		╱
▽	434		◺	
▲	435	◺		
◐	436	◺		
◉	437	◺		
▼	522	◺	⊙	
	632			╱
★	640	◺		
◉	642	◺		
–	644	◺		
C	676	◺		
	726		▣	
▨	729	⬚		
▽	738	◺		
	741		◆	
	742		*	
	760		▲	
	761		◉	
◖	780	◺	▣	
H	782	◺	▢	
T	783	◺	▣	
·	822	·	·	
◉	898			
■	902	◺		▱
	926		⊠	
	927		☆	
	935		▣	╱
	938			╱
▨	950	◪		
	3046		2	
	3047		◉	
▣	3328	◺		
■	3362	◺	▣	╱
	3363		★	╱
‖	3364	◺	▽	
	3713		8	
2	3722	◺		
	3768		▼	
=	3773	◺		
◇	3774	◺		
U	3787	◺		╱
V	3823	◺		
	3828		▣	
◉	3362	French Knot		

STITCH COUNT (61w x 80h)

14 count	4³⁄₈"	x	5³⁄₄"
16 count	3⁷⁄₈"	x	5"
18 count	3¹⁄₂"	x	4¹⁄₂"
22 count	2⁷⁄₈"	x	3³⁄₄"

Harvesttime in Frame (shown on page 43): The design was stitched over 2 fabric threads on a 13" x 14" piece of Platinum Cashel Linen® (28 ct). Three strands of floss were used for Cross Stitch and 1 strand for Half Cross Stitch, Backstitch, and French Knots. It was custom framed.

Needlework adaptation by Donna Vermillion Giampa.

CANTICLE OF BROTHER SUN

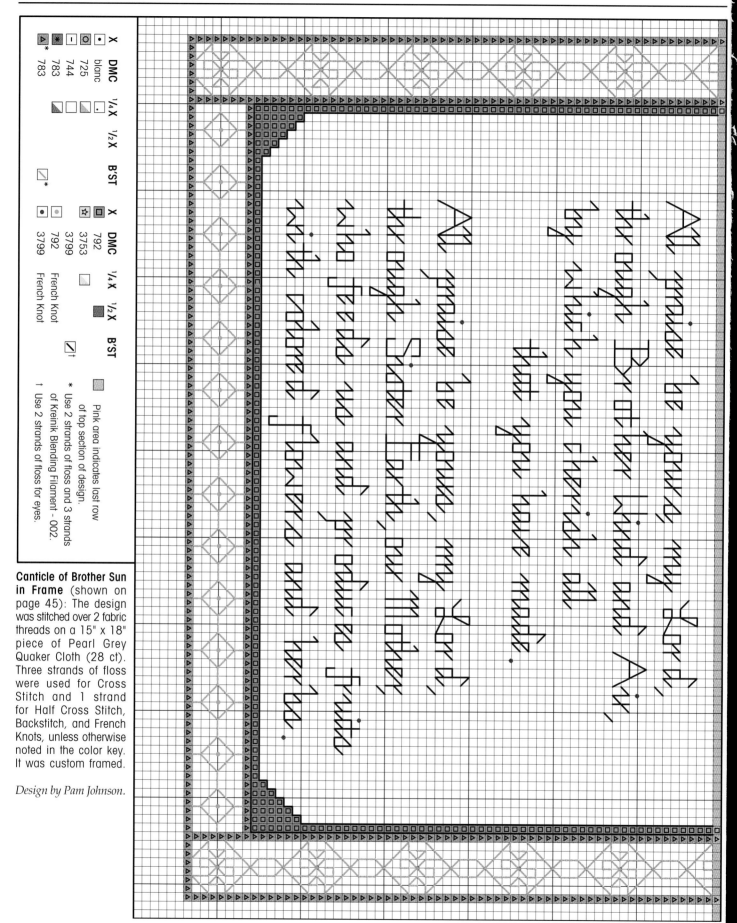

Canticle of Brother Sun in Frame (shown on page 45): The design was stitched over 2 fabric threads on a 15" x 18" piece of Pearl Grey Quaker Cloth (28 ct). Three strands of floss were used for Cross Stitch and 1 strand for Half Cross Stitch, Backstitch, and French Knots, unless otherwise noted in the color key. It was custom framed.

Design by Pam Johnson.

Canticle of Brother Sun

All praise be yours, my Lord,
through Brother Sun
who brings the day and light.

All praise be yours, my Lord,
through Sister Moon and Stars
In the heavens you have made them...

100w x 140h

93

the lord's prayer

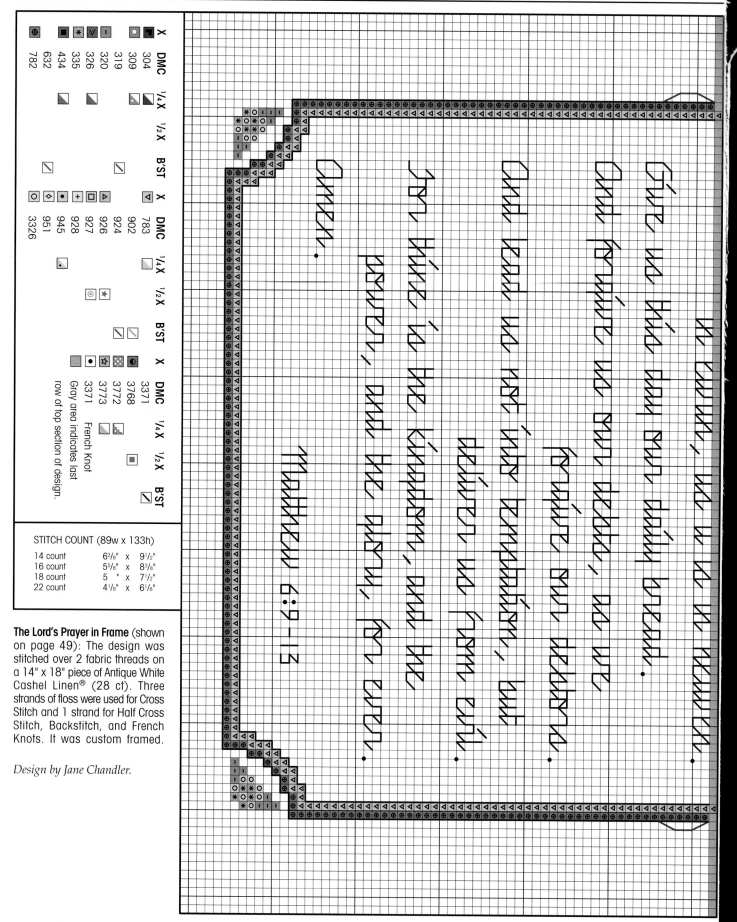

X	1/4X	1/2X	B'ST	DMC
				304
				309
				319
				320
				326
				335
				434
				632
				782

X	1/4X	1/2X	B'ST	DMC
				783
				902
				924
				926
				927
				928
				945
				951
				3326

X	1/4X	1/2X	B'ST	DMC
				3371
				3768
				3772
				3773

French Knot

Gray area indicates last row of top section of design.

STITCH COUNT (89w x 133h)

14 count	6 3/8"	x 9 1/2"
16 count	5 5/8"	x 8 3/8"
18 count	5 "	x 7 1/2"
22 count	4 1/8"	x 6 1/8"

The Lord's Prayer in Frame (shown on page 49): The design was stitched over 2 fabric threads on a 14" x 18" piece of Antique White Cashel Linen® (28 ct). Three strands of floss were used for Cross Stitch and 1 strand for Half Cross Stitch, Backstitch, and French Knots. It was custom framed.

Design by Jane Chandler.

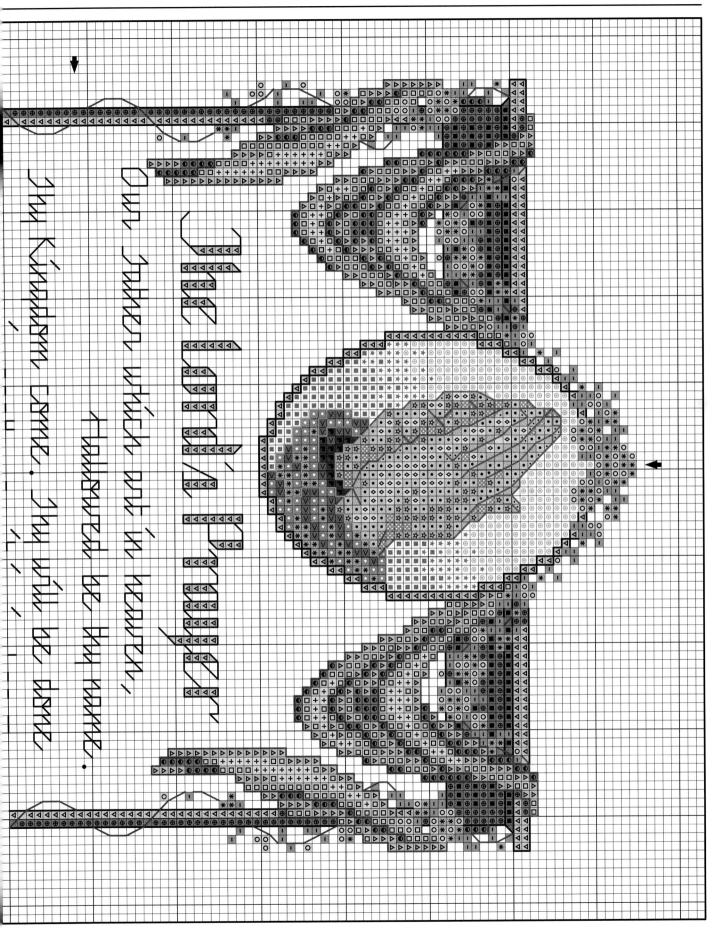

GENERAL INSTRUCTIONS

WORKING WITH CHARTS

How to Read Charts: Each of the designs is shown in chart form. Each colored square on the chart represents one Cross Stitch or one Half Cross Stitch. Each colored triangle on the chart represents one One-Quarter Stitch or one Three-Quarter Stitch. In some charts, reduced symbols are used to indicate One-Quarter Stitches and Three-Quarter Stitches (**Fig. 1**). **Fig. 2** and **Fig. 3** indicate Cross Stitch under Backstitch.

Fig. 1   **Fig. 2**   **Fig. 3**

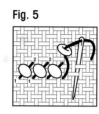

Black or colored dots on the chart represent Cross Stitch, French Knots, or bead placement. The black or colored straight lines on the chart indicate Backstitch. The symbol is omitted or reduced when a French Knot or Backstitch covers a square.

Each chart is accompanied by a color key. This key indicates the color of floss to use for each stitch on the chart. The headings on the color key are for Cross Stitch (**X**), DMC color number (**DMC**), One-Quarter Stitch (**¼X**), Three-Quarter Stitch (**¾X**), Half Cross Stitch (**½X**), and Backstitch (**B'ST**). Color key columns should be read vertically and horizontally to determine type of stitch and floss color. Some designs may include stitches worked with metallic thread, such as Blending Filament, Braid, or Cable. The metallic thread may be blended with floss or used alone. If any metallic thread is used in a design, the color key will contain the necessary information.

STITCHING TIPS

Working over Two Fabric Threads: Use the sewing method instead of the stab method when working over two fabric threads. To use the sewing method, keep your stitching hand on the right side of the fabric (instead of stabbing the fabric with the needle and taking your stitching hand to the back of the fabric to pick up the needle). With the sewing method, you take the needle down and up with one stroke instead of two. To add support to stitches, it is important that the first Cross Stitch be placed on the fabric with stitch 1-2 beginning and ending where a vertical fabric thread crosses over a horizontal fabric thread (**Fig. 4**). When the first stitch is in the correct position, the entire design will be placed properly, with vertical fabric threads supporting each stitch.

Fig. 4

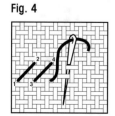

Attaching Beads: Refer to chart for bead placement and sew bead in place using a fine needle that will pass through bead. Bring needle up at 1, run needle through bead and then down at 2. Secure floss on back or move to next bead as shown in **Fig. 5**.

Fig. 5

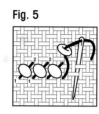

STITCH DIAGRAMS

Note: Bring threaded needle up at 1 and all odd numbers and down at 2 and all even numbers.

Counted Cross Stitch (X): Work one Cross Stitch to correspond to each colored square on the chart. For horizontal rows, work stitches in two journeys (**Fig. 6**). For vertical rows, complete each stitch as shown (**Fig. 7**). When working over two fabric threads, work Cross Stitch as shown in **Fig. 8**. When the chart shows a Backstitch crossing a colored square (**Fig. 9**), a Cross Stitch should be worked first; then the Backstitch (**Fig. 14** or **15**) should be worked on top of the Cross Stitch.

Fig. 6   **Fig. 7**

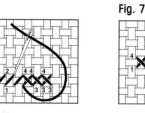

Fig. 8   **Fig. 9**

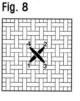

Quarter Stitch (¼X and ¾X): Quarter Stitches are denoted by triangular shapes of color on the chart and on the color key. For a One-Quarter Stitch, come up at 1 (**Fig. 10**), then split fabric thread to go down at 2. When stitches 1-4 are worked in the same color, the resulting stitch is called a Three-Quarter Stitch (**¾X**). **Fig. 11** shows the technique for Quarter Stitches when working over two fabric threads.

Fig. 10   **Fig. 11**

Half Cross Stitch (½X): This stitch is o~~~ journey of the Cross Stitch and is worked fr~~~ lower left to upper right as shown ~~~ **Fig. 12**. When working over two fabric threa~~~ work Half Cross Stitch as shown in **Fig. 13**.

Fig. 12   **Fig. 13**

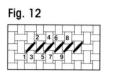

Backstitch (B'ST): For outline detail, Backstit~~~ (shown on chart and on color key by black ~~~ colored straight lines) should be worked after t~~~ design has been completed (**Fig. 14**). Whe~~~ working over two fabric threads, work Backstit~~~ as shown in **Fig. 15**.

Fig. 14   **Fig. 15**

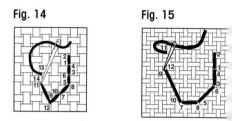

French Knot: Bring needle up at 1. Wrap flo~~~ once around needle and insert needle ~~~ 2, holding end of floss with non-stitching finge~~~ (**Fig. 16**). Tighten knot, then pull needle throu~~~ fabric, holding floss until it must be release~~~ For larger knot, use more strands of floss; wr~~~ only once.

Fig. 16

Instructions tested and photo items made by L~~~ Allen, Marsha Besancon, Karen Brogan, Vanes~~~ Edwards, Jody Fuller, Elaine Garrett, Diana Hoke, ~~~ Johnson, Wanda J. Linsley, Melanie Long, Phy~~~ Lundy, Karen Matthew, Susan McDonald, Jill Morg~~~ Martha Nolan, Patricia O'Neil, Angie Perryman, Jo~~~ Robinson, Laura Rowan, Cynthia Sanders, Sus~~~ Sego, Lavonne Sims, Lorissa Smith, Amy Tayl~~~ Karen Tyler, Trish Vines, Andrea Westbrook, ~~~ Janice Williams.